Praise for *Si...*

"I have known David Ash for ten years. I have seen him as an investor and a steward of wealth; he doesn't just talk about these principles, he applies them himself—with consistency and discipline. *Simple Wealth* is a checklist of sound investing principles, forged by experiences from the backstreets of Montreal to the streets of some of the world's financial centers."

BEN SLAGER, founding partner, Mogan Daniels Slager LLP; M&A, private equity, venture capital, commercial law; co-chair, TIGER 21 (Vancouver)

"As I read David Ash's book, I kept having a recurring thought: *My four adult kids need to read this book; My friends need to read this book; I'm going to recommend this book to _____!* I believe in David and in his hard-won financial expertise. He speaks the truth, gives attainable, practical advice, and presents it in an easy-to-read format. This book will help you!"

BRENT CANTELON, pastor, Brent Cantelon Ministries

"David Ash has a great way of taking complex ideas and distilling them into easy-to-understand concepts that are practical and thought-provoking. *Simple Wealth* is a tool that anyone can use to build a better life."

CRAIG FAULKNER, chief technology officer, Unilogik Systems Inc.

"'Keep it simple' is the message you will take away from *Simple Wealth*. An easy-to-follow roadmap to financial freedom—and a must-read for my adult sons. David Ash is a visionary with a heart for people."

FRANCO PAPALIA, portfolio manager, Raymond James

"Why aren't more books written like this? Easy to read and to the point. *Simple Wealth* is based on real stories and experiences that will impact your life quickly and significantly. Just *wow*... an easy, thoughtful gift to give to people I care about!"

FRED MERCER, multi-unit franchise owner, Expedia Cruises

"If you have had money, want to have money, have lost money, or have made lots of money, this book is for you. It is easy to read and full of simple, down-home financial wisdom. *Simple Wealth* translates decades of David Ash's wins and losses into humble, deep wisdom on how to handle money—and keep it from handling you."

LARRY BIRCHALL, executive chairman, Longbow Capital Inc.

"In this increasingly complex and rapidly changing world, it's refreshing to come across a salient, succinct, and simple yet effective formula for financial freedom. One that demonstrates we don't all have to work for Google or be doctors to gain that freedom; that with a little discipline today, we can all achieve the peace of mind that comes with financial security. In *Simple Wealth*, David Ash has outlined, for young and old alike, the formula that has always existed, but has been largely forgotten in this age of immediate gratification. He reminds us that the key to financial independence is the disciplined application of simple rules over time."

PAUL GREHAN, founder, Rybridge Capital

"*Simple Wealth* is not a book—it is a *manual*! David Ash has done a spectacular job distilling myriad elements that represent an overwhelming complexity for many of us. Simmering the process of financial freedom down to Six Proven Principles takes unparalleled skill. This book is easy to read, relatable, and contains real action points—kudos!"

ROXANA COLQUHOUN, cofounder, HNW Services Inc.; chair, TIGER 21 (BC)

"*Simple Wealth* is one of the most profound books I have read on the subject of wealth creation. David Ash doesn't just talk the talk, he walks the walk. Everyone needs to read this book."

NIGEL BENNETT, founder, Aqua-Guard Spill Response, TruBeach, and giftADD.com; author, *Take That Leap: Risking It All for What Really Matters*

"In *Simple Wealth*, David Ash provides a clear, concise, and practical guide for the journey to financial independence—and the wealth of opportunities this can bring to virtually anyone. David has generously shared experiences from his own life that serve as examples of how financial success can be achieved by following some simple but critically important truths. He appropriately warns us not to be fooled by the simplicity of timeless truths, as 'truth is always simple.' *Simple Wealth* is a perfect embodiment of this principle."

TIMOTHY DANIELS, CEO, TIGER 21

"I thoroughly enjoyed reading *Simple Wealth* and have had a ringside seat watching David Ash put these principles into practice. His life is living proof that these methods work. As Brian Tracy says, 'Success leaves tracks'—there's no reason to reinvent the wheel, just follow those tracks!"

PRAVEEN VARSHNEY, FCPA, FCA, director, Varshney Capital Corp.

Simple Wealth

DAVID ASH

Simple
Wealth

SIX PROVEN PRINCIPLES
FOR FINANCIAL FREEDOM

PAGE TWO
BOOKS

Cataloguing in publication information is available from Library and Archives Canada.
ISBN 978-1-77458-010-3 (paperback)
ISBN 978-1-77458-011-0 (ebook)

Page Two
www.pagetwo.com

Edited by Kendra Ward
Copyedited by Crissy Calhoun
Proofread by Alison Strobel
Cover design by Taysia Louie
Interior design by Fiona Lee

simplewealthbooks.com

*This book is dedicated to my son, Donavon,
and my daughter, Jasmine—my pride and joy.*

Contents

Introduction

————

I N THE SPRING of 1989, I was at the lowest point of my young
life. My bank accounts were empty, unpaid bills were
piling up, and I was seven years behind on my income
taxes. I wanted to run and hide, but I had no money and
nowhere to go.

So, at the age of twenty-eight, I filed for bankruptcy.

My journey to this heartbreaking conclusion had begun
ten years earlier with such promise, when, as a young real
estate agent, I attended a sales seminar. That day was
the first time I had heard the words *positive*, *mental*, and
attitude used together and expressed as a concept. The
unbridled optimism I experienced in that meeting gave
me a new hope. The kind my father, who had worked on
a loading dock, and my mother, a nurse's assistant, never
had. I left that conference with an armload of books and
tapes and then sat alone in my little apartment late into
the night, listening, reading, and dreaming.

The books I read and the tapes I listened to all spoke
of the need to set clear, measurable goals far beyond

anything you could reasonably imagine achieving. My heart ached for a better life. So, safe in the darkness of my basement suite, I pushed away the whispers of self-doubt, rebelled against reason, and set my first major goal: "I will be a millionaire by the age of thirty." I taped this incredible proclamation to my bathroom mirror, stood at attention, and defiantly declared it in the morning and night. My future was bright; I believed anything was possible.

Over the next ten years, I worked long and hard. I gave it everything I had, but it wasn't enough. The millionaire at thirty was bankrupt at twenty-eight.

If you are a lawyer and you declare bankruptcy, you are still a lawyer. If you are a twenty-eight-year-old high school dropout and you declare bankruptcy, you are broke, desperate, and afraid.

The only bright spot in my life at that time was a beautiful nurse, my future wife, Lise. I remember coming home from a meeting with a bankruptcy trustee one day and, with tears in my eyes, telling Lise that she deserved better, that she should leave me and marry a doctor or a lawyer. Surprised and offended, she said she didn't want a doctor or a lawyer; she wanted me. I loved Lise enough to let her go that day, and she loved me enough to stay.

The upside to bankruptcy is that it gives you time and space to reflect. I had started out as a salesman, became a sales manager, and then an entrepreneur. Along the way, I had learned how to set goals, drive revenue, and get everyone moving in the same direction. What I didn't like or respect was the discipline of money management and bookkeeping. I had focused on the top-line sales and revenue, assuming the bottom line would take care of itself.

At this most critical time in my life when I was looking for a new way forward, I remembered a little paperback I had read ten years earlier that I thought might help me: *The Richest Man in Babylon* was written by George S. Clason in 1926—almost one hundred years ago now. As I read the short stories and parables again, I was transported back in time to the dusty streets of the ancient city, where I sat at the feet of the richest man in Babylon with chariot builders and minstrels. Clason's words filled my heart with the hopes and dreams I had lost along the way. I saw a new way up and out of the mess I was in. But I knew I couldn't do it alone.

When I sheepishly approached Lise with my head down and the book in my hand, I didn't know how she would respond. "I was a nurse," she recalled recently. "I had no interest in being wealthy, but these ideas made sense to me. They gave us direction and promised stability, and that made me feel safe. I saw David commit to us that day and I married him in my heart."

My young nurse's response speaks to the deeply personal and complex relationship we all have with money. Few subjects strike as close to the heart of who we are—how much we have, earn, give away, or keep—as it does. Money can make us feel happy, sad, hopeful, fearful, discouraged, generous, or greedy. Marriages break up; wars are fought; people strike, protest, riot, and go to prison over it. People starve or become homeless because of the lack of it. Charities, hospitals, and churches all need money to care for our emotional, physical, and spiritual needs. The Bible says more about money, and our relationship with it, than it does about any other subject. Money is a lot of things, but one thing it is clearly not is unimportant.

From *The Richest Man in Babylon*, Lise and I learned that "wealth [is] like a tree" and that every dollar we saved would be a seed for a new tree.[1] So, we started by applying the first and most important of Clason's golden rules and saving 10% of all we earned, no matter what.

The first $100 we saved in 1989 was our first feeble step in the right direction. We had no way of knowing then how true the words we read in that little book really were. Today I am a full-time investor. With the help of a small but highly qualified management team, we own and manage a large portfolio of income-producing real estate and other investments. The steady stream of rental revenue and dividends we earn has been our sole source of income since 2004. Our financial independence has given us the freedom to travel the world and support the charitable work we care most about. It has also allowed us to help friends, family, and random strangers in need along the way. Most surprising of all, our net worth has more than doubled in that time.

A Better Way for a Rainy Day

WHEN I first considered writing this book, like any good investor, I counted the cost. I knew it would require hundreds of hours of alone time, reflecting and writing. I finally decided to take on the project for two reasons. The first is that I am a father. I may not be around to mentor my children, or their children, when they need me the most. When rainy days roll in—as they do from time to time—and they ask, "What would Dad do?" they will know. I have also written this book for anyone who is feeling as lost or trapped as I was thirty years ago. I know how fearful and desperate you are feeling. Take heart: there is a way up and out of the mess you are in.

This book is divided into four parts. Part One, A Unique Form of Intelligence, argues that true financial intelligence is more about persistence, determination, self-awareness, and self-control than it is about academic achievement or IQ. That no matter who you are or where you are from, you can live a life filled with options and opportunities instead of regrets and debts. Part Two, The Six Proven Principles for Financial Freedom, explores the universal principles that govern the creation and management of wealth and how anyone living anywhere—rich, poor, or bankrupt—can apply them. In Part Three, Financially Intelligent Investing, you will discover powerful proven strategies that work for know-nothing investors that will outperform professional money managers most of the time.

With the changing job market, more people are starting businesses than ever before. Owning and operating your own business can be the single greatest wealth generator there is. Entrepreneurs enjoy a creative freedom and independence they would not have working for someone else. However, the transition from employee to employer is not without its risks. Unforeseen circumstances, or rogue waves, can appear out of nowhere, wiping out years of hard work for the unprepared. Part Four, The Financially Intelligent Entrepreneur, looks at the realities of business ownership and shows readers how to protect and manage their *personal* financial lives, while still pursuing their entrepreneurial dreams.

Countless financial experts and writers have squeezed their thesauruses dry over the years trying to communicate these same ideas in new and compelling ways. The reason I am joining this parade of advice-givers is that these principles work. They have transformed my life, and they will transform yours, if you let them.

I offer only one caution. As you read these timeless truths, do not be fooled by their simplicity. Truth is always simple.

AS LISE and I brought Clason's golden rules into our lives, our confidence grew with our bank balances, and we began sharing what we had learned with friends, people going through tough times of their own. We even bought some of them a copy of our favorite little book. In the early years, we always took comfort in the knowledge that we had made a difference in our friends' lives. However, our excitement often gave way to confusion when, over time, we discovered that some of them had done little or nothing to change. Since then, we have met people from all walks of life, many highly educated professionals, who struggle the same way our friends have. Their homes and cars may be bigger, but their problems are the same.

So why have some of our friends and so many others ignored these common-sense principles that changed our lives? Is there a unique form of intelligence—a financial intelligence, or FQ—that some people have and others don't?

I believe there is.

PART ONE

A Unique Form of Intelligence

"One of psychology's open secrets is
the relative inability of grades, IQ, or SAT scores,
despite their popular mystique, to predict
unerringly who will succeed in life."

DANIEL GOLEMAN, *EMOTIONAL INTELLIGENCE*

1

Academic Achievement
Is Being Oversold

THE IDEA THAT there might be a unique form of intelligence that some people have, and others don't, occurred to me for the first time as a young real estate agent knocking on doors in a predominantly Italian neighborhood. I was often invited in to discuss property values and market conditions.

The perfectly maintained red-brick homes I sat in always had immaculately manicured lawns, beautifully trimmed hedges, and vegetable gardens bursting with juicy Roma tomatoes. Every one of these little castles was filled with generations of family photos, from the old country and the new. I always enjoyed the lively conversations, in broken English, and the homemade wine the families plied me with. But I often stumbled out of these meetings more confused than I had been when I went in. How had these warm-hearted immigrants managed to buy a home and two duplexes around the corner, while my parents struggled financially and paid rent their whole lives?

What did they know that we didn't?

As I shared this story with a good friend of mine, Franco, a sly smile slowly crossed his face. His family's story offers us some clues.

Franco's father, Carmelo, was born in 1925 in the tiny sunbaked village of Taurianova in the Calabria region of southern Italy. Orphaned at the age of two, he was taken in by his sickly grandmother. Being the only "man" in the house, Carmelo was forced to care for his nonna through the Great Depression and the Second World War. These responsibilities, and the harsh realities of the world he lived in, left no time for formal education.

In 1945, at the age of twenty, Carmelo finally caught a break when a fortunate relative sponsored his immigration to Vancouver, British Columbia. Arriving penniless, he moved in with relatives and, through a friend, quickly secured employment with a gas company, digging ditches for gas lines. Once settled, Carmelo sent a letter home to Taurianova with news of his good fortune and proposed marriage to his childhood sweetheart, Angela Rosa.

Newly married, with a wife to care for and a life to build, Carmelo worked long and hard, digging ditches for the gas company. He never refused overtime, and it was offered a lot. Over the years, Carmelo and Angela Rosa saved and, when they could, invested Carmelo's earnings in real estate. They had five boys, each born one year apart, and as devout Catholics believed that God had blessed their marriage with children. By the age of forty-five, twenty-five years after landing in Canada as a penniless immigrant, the family owned five duplexes, clear title.

Tired of the long days, and with his financial future finally secure, Carmelo felt safe taking a less demanding job in a warehouse. Life was good and the family's future was bright, until tragedy struck. Shortly after taking the job, Carmelo was killed in a work-related accident: a fork-lift fell over on him in the warehouse. Angela Rosa was left alone, dressed in black, to mourn the love of her life and raise her growing boys.

Franco says that the income from those five duplexes is what his mother used to raise them. Without it, she would have been forced into some form of low-paying labor. Instead, she was able to stay home, as she always had, and care for her boys.

Franco's mother passed away recently at the age of ninety. She still owned the five duplexes. The only thing that changed over the years was their value.

Angela Rosa was worth over $12 million.

Franco's father could not have predicted what the properties he had worked so hard to buy and pay off would mean to his family one day. He also may not have known what an IQ test or SAT score was. But he had qualities that were far more important. He was a good father, husband, and a member of his community. Plus, he was motivated, persistent, determined, and humble. He had self-awareness, self-control, and the ability to delay gratification; he knew the value of short-term sacrifice for long-term gain. These are all qualities that psychologist and bestselling author Dr. Daniel Goleman describes as emotional intelligence. Goleman became interested in what he saw as a narrow view of intelligence. He acknowledges that there is a relationship between IQ and how someone's life turns out. People with low IQs often end up in low-paying, menial jobs and people with high IQs sometimes end up in well-paying jobs. But he points out that this is not always the case: "At best, IQ contributes about 20 percent to the factors that determine life success, which leaves 80 percent to other forces."[1]

Goleman believes academic intelligence is being over-sold, that there is an overemphasis in academia, and society in general, on IQ as a predictor of success. He concludes, "People with high IQs can be stunningly poor pilots of their personal lives."[2]

Grades, IQ, or SAT scores cannot accurately predict a person's chance of living a full and meaningful life.

I WISHED I had a copy of Goleman's book *Emotional Intelligence* with me at my son's hockey practice, back in 2008. I was at the Sportsplex near my family's home. The facility, which has four arenas, a gym, a hockey shop, daycare centers, and a concession, was a beehive of activity that morning. It is home to minor hockey teams, beer leagues, and figure skating clubs. It is a big part of the community we live in.

As I stood watching my boy bang and crash into the boards, I couldn't help but think of how far we had come as a family over the last twenty years. Starting with nothing in 1989, Lise and I had embraced a new way of life, together, following the principles laid out in *The Richest Man in Babylon*. Of course, there were challenges along the way, but in the end, we had landed on our feet in spectacular fashion.

As I blew the steam off my coffee, I was lost in these pleasant thoughts, when the loud, angry words of an unpleasant woman standing near me jolted me back to reality. She was shaking her head, going on and on, complaining loudly and bitterly to a friend about her son. "I've told Tommy he has to get better grades, or he is not going to go anywhere in life!"

I knew Tommy. He was my son's friend and a good kid.

Not going to go anywhere in life! Her unkind words rang in my ears. How dare she publicly sentence her own son to such a fate? I suddenly felt like the little boy I had been in elementary school, disciplined and ostracized. I felt like I had been slapped. The hair on the back of my neck stood up and my eyes narrowed. Everything in me wanted to lean in and interrupt her conversation. To defend her son, myself, and every other child who struggles in school. But I knew that conversation would not go well. So, fuming, I shook my head, bit my tongue, and moved away. I didn't tell her that she should read Goleman's book on emotional intelligence. Or that the high school dropout standing next to her owned the arena she was standing in.

TO BE perfectly clear, I am a huge fan of education and have deep admiration for anyone who has a high IQ and is gifted academically. Goleman's point, and I agree, is that these qualities alone offer no guarantee of success, financial or otherwise. Knowledge for the sake of knowledge is worthless. Franco's father didn't need a university education to know that he had to live on less than he earned and save for the future, no matter what. He embraced the idea of short-term sacrifice for long-term gain and knew the

difference between needs and wants. His family lived fru-
gally, but well, and borrowed money from no one. Franco's
mother had a beautiful vegetable garden in the backyard
that fed them all. Everything was made from scratch, just
like in the old country. The smell of delicious homemade
bread, pasta, and wine often filled the house. They went
out for dinner as a family only once a year. Angela Rosa
made or mended all their clothes. Franco and his four
brothers, the unpaid laborers, painted, cut grass, and
otherwise maintained their growing portfolio of rental
properties, all of which were situated within a two-block
radius. Organized sports were out of the question: too
expensive. Street hockey in front of the house was their
favorite pastime. Franco says they never felt hard done by.

Just like the real estate clients I drank homemade wine
with, Carmelo understood the Six Proven Principles for
Financial Freedom. He knew he had to:

1   *Save* a percentage of all he earned
2   *Control* his expenses
3   Make his money *multiply*
4   *Protect* his wealth from loss
5   *Own* a home
6   *Increase* his ability to earn

So, he stuck to investments that he understood and
could control: duplexes in his own neighborhood. Assets
that would go up in value over time and provide an income
for the future.

Carmelo had true financial intelligence.

A SIMPLE SUMMARY

- True financial intelligence, or your FQ, is a combination of age-old financial wisdom and knowledge, guided by a healthy dose of emotional intelligence—which is a macro-ability or life compass.

- Your levels of emotional and financial intelligence can be increased and developed over time.

- Academic achievement is not a predictor of success.

2

Never Underestimate the Resolve of the Underdog

O F COURSE, WE are not all created equally. Some of us are stronger, faster, or smarter than others. Some of us have been born into families that have loved, supported, and encouraged us to be all that we can be. Some have not. The good news is that success is not about what you have or don't have, or the family you are from. It's *what you do with what you have* that counts most in life.

My friend Lance is a prime example. Born in 1956 and raised in a tar-paper shack with no running water or electricity, he was part of a hillbilly clan, complete with moonshining and feuding. Lance worked the family farm, hunted, and fished from the time he could walk. He was a sharpshooter and had "bagged his first deer" at the age of seven. Lance's father had abandoned the family when he was young. His mother was illiterate. The only member of the extended family who could read was his grandmother, who was an apparent authority on all subjects.

Reader's Digest was her bible—she had stacks of them piled everywhere.

In the late 1920s, Lance's American grandparents, Archie and Renee, had followed logging roads up into Washington State mountain wilderness in search of free land and a better way of life. What they didn't know then, and only discovered years later when a government surveyor showed up, was that their homestead was not in the United States at all but three miles north of the 49th parallel, in British Columbia, Canada. Overnight, the only logging road into their settlement became a border crossing, and they became Canadians.

None of the children attended school and the adults made no attempt at homeschooling. All of that changed when a reporter heard about the hillbilly colony trapped in the mountains. Their incredible story, complete with family photos, was front-page news. Lance showed me a copy of an article from the 1960s that he found at the library. Hollywood could not have assembled a better cast of characters. His mother, in rumpled coveralls, is standing, unsmiling, next to her four scruffy children, holding the rifle she went everywhere with. Lance recalls being confused when he saw the family photo. He didn't recognize himself—they didn't own a mirror.

This sudden media attention led to a visit from a social worker, who told Lance's mother that her children had to go to school, that it was required by law. Trapped in the hills without roads linking them to any Canadian communities, Lance and his siblings had to walk about an hour through the bush, down the canyon, across the creek, up the other side, and then along a trail to meet the gravel road where they would then take the bus nine miles to school in Chilliwack.

The four siblings all started grade one together. The youngest was six, the oldest was nine, Lance was seven. Encountering civilization in a grade one classroom must have been a surreal experience for the poor, illiterate mountain children. Lance ended up floating through the school system until he dropped out in grade nine, still unable to read a restaurant menu. After run-ins with the law, a short stay in a juvenile detention center, and a series of dead-end jobs, his future was looking no better than his past.

Finally, at the age of twenty-one, he resolved to learn how to read. Literacy opened the door to a whole new world of opportunities for Lance. In 1980, he got a job selling photocopiers and something that was revolutionary at that time: personal computers. Knocking on doors, Lance discovered that many businesses wanted one of his new machines, but few people knew how to use one. Business 101 courses talk about finding a need and filling it, and that's what Lance did. He started his own computer training school.

Timing, as they say, is everything. His new business grew quickly; he grabbed market share and kept it. Lance ran his business profitably for twenty years before retiring early and wealthy.

It's doubtful that Lance would have scored anywhere near average on an IQ test as a teenager. Illiteracy, poverty, and relative isolation had created a set of seemingly insurmountable obstacles for him, and by most standards they were. But these outward conditions don't tell the whole story.

Living in the hills without electricity and running water and surviving through subsistence-level farming, hunting, fishing, and bartering required persistence, determination, and self-discipline. It required the ability to delay gratification and a level of motivation not needed by most city folk. After learning how to read, Lance focused these same qualities of character, his emotional intelligence, on whatever goals he set for himself, and he succeeded.

And you can too.

A SIMPLE SUMMARY

- You are not defined by your past.

- Success in life is not about what you have. It's what you *do* with what you *have* that counts.

- Focused persistence is unstoppable.

3

A Partial Truth Is
No Truth at All

_____

DON'T LIKE BEING called a liar. Especially by someone I barely know, in public. But that is exactly what happened to me at a conference in Boston. I was enjoying dinner with a group of young entrepreneurs when the topic of what we thought drove us to succeed came up, and I said, "I think I am motivated because I come from nothing."

The gentleman sitting across from me looked me straight in the eye and said, "I think that's bull..."

The table was stunned into silence, and I wasn't smiling. My candid colleague took this pregnant pause as an opportunity to elaborate. "I come from a wealthy family. My dad was a successful entrepreneur. When I graduated from high school, he wrote me a check for $1 million and said, 'Here is your start in life.'"

He went on to explain that he took his windfall, bought a nice old Camaro, and used the balance to put himself through university. After graduating with a computer science degree, at the height of the dot-com boom, he and a classmate started a consulting firm. They had just sold that company for millions and he was planning a sailboat adventure around the world with his wife and children.

When I thought more deeply about my dinner companion's observation, I appreciated the risk he took by being honest. I wasn't being honest with myself. Laziness and ambition are alive and well at all levels of the socioeconomic ladder. My reasoning was nothing more than a romantic cliché. A story I had been subconsciously telling myself my whole life was based on a partial truth, which is no truth at all.

We are complex beings and the way we respond to the world around us is shaped by the generational forces of our family, culture, and socioeconomic backgrounds. The reasons we think and act the way we do are as complicated as we are. But they don't have to define us.

Financial psychologist Bradley Klontz and his partner Sonya Britt have made this subject the focus of their research at Kansas State University and have developed an online predictive tool that helps people better understand their financial behavior.[1] Their studies suggest we all operate from one of four money scripts: avoidance, worship, status, and vigilance.

AVOIDANCE

Avoiders believe that money is bad or that they do not deserve money. Money is viewed as a source of fear, anxiety, or disgust. Avoiders believe people of wealth are greedy and corrupt, that there is virtue in living with less. Avoiders sometimes struggle with conflicting beliefs that money could end their problems and that wealth is contemptible, while at the same time placing too much value on money related to their own life satisfaction.

WORSHIP

Money worshippers believe that money is the key to happiness and the solution to all of their problems but that they can never really have enough. And yet the pursuit of money never fully satisfies them. This tension sometimes leads to overspending in an attempt to buy happiness. Hoarding, excessive debt, and workaholism are possible negative side effects of money worship.

STATUS

Money status seekers see net worth and self-worth as synonymous. They may pretend to have more money than they do and, as a result, overspend. They believe people are as successful as the amount of money they have.

VIGILANCE

The money vigilant are alert, watchful, and concerned about their financial welfare. They believe it is important to save and for people to work for their money. If they can't pay cash for something, they won't buy it. They also tend to be anxious and secretive about their financial status, apart from those closest to them.

Klontz and Britt believe these scripts are deeply rooted, culturally bound, and inherited.

Like a movie script, your financial script is the story you tell yourself about money and your relationship with it. Knowing what you really think and feel, and why, is the first step in developing a healthy money mindset.

The Legacy of Avoidance

I GREW up in working-class neighborhoods in the west end of Montreal. Always tenants, my family rented a small three-bedroom apartment in a three-block neighborhood of identical, interconnected buildings. My friends and I could run from one end of the street to the other on the roofs, if we didn't get caught. Our primary playgrounds were streets, back alleys, and factory fields.

I remember playing on the loading dock of the milk-bottling plant across the street. It had two large conveyor chains in the concrete floor that were constantly running out of the plant onto the loading dock with crates of milk and cream for the waiting trucks. One afternoon we spontaneously decided to stand on the conveyor chains to see where they would take us. I'll never forget the shocked looks and conspiratorial grins on the faces of the hard men working the bottling machines as three scruffy, wide-eyed eight-year-old boys slid slowly by, grinning from ear to ear on a private tour of their plant. No one raised the alarm.

The freedom we had to move about as children of the sixties was wonderful. For ten cents, we could take a thirty-minute bus ride downtown. This journey took us through progressively more affluent neighborhoods along the way. I remember staring out the window at the well-maintained, red-brick character homes perched on sloping manicured lawns lined with huge maple, oak, and weeping willow trees. The soft, quiet, safe feeling of these wide, tree-lined streets and the oasis-like parks was in stark contrast to the forest of balconies and cracked sidewalks we played on. Although I loved the neighborhood I grew up in, I could not escape the idea that the clean, neat, happy-looking people that lived in these affluent neighborhoods were better than us.

I am sure that this idea was subtly reinforced by my parents, who shared a money avoidance script that supported the ideas that they didn't deserve money and that wealthy people were greedy and corrupt. My parents saw money as a source of fear, anxiety, and disgust. They were children of the Great Depression. My mother, an orphan, had been a ward of the court. A foster child who bounced from home to home in some of the poorest neighborhoods of the city. She learned to survive by her wits, working the "system" whenever she could. At the age of thirteen, she finally caught a break and was taken in by an affluent family in the suburbs. But by that time, the damage was done.

My father came from a large, loving, church-going family. However, at thirteen years old, he was encouraged to drop out of school to help support his nine brothers and sisters. He went to work in a paint factory, soldering the tops onto paint cans. "Made $8 a week, brought $6 home, kept $2 for myself," he reminded my brothers and me often. My father took blue-collar pride in working long and hard, for almost nothing.

The instability and deprivation of my mother's childhood had left her with a deeply rooted poverty mentality anchored in a fear and distrust of authority. While my parents' backgrounds were different, they shared an unspoken suspicion and resentment for the rich. Their definition of *rich* was never clear, but as a child I sensed that it included anyone who owned a home and lived in a nice neighborhood.

Perception Is Not Always Reality

IN RETROSPECT, it's easy to see that my family's financial issues were more about perception than reality. My father had a union job with the railway and my mother, when she was well enough to work, was a nurse's assistant. There was always food on the table, clothes on our backs, and presents under the Christmas tree. I had friends in my neighborhood from large single-parent families living on social assistance. They were poor; we were not.

As a young man, I rejected the hopelessness and despair that marked the poverty mentality I was raised with. There was a better future on the other side of town. I saw wealth as a cure-all, and I was prepared to go where I had to go and take whatever risk I had to take to get there. I put everything aside in favor of my pursuit of wealth. I had no hobbies or interests beyond partying on the weekends to blow off steam from the workweek. I had developed an unhealthy money worship script.

Klontz and Britt also believe that some people operate from a curious blend of more than one money script. I think this might explain why I feel the way I do in certain circumstances. One sunny Sunday afternoon drive with my family serves as a perfect example. As we drove past a yacht club in a nice part of town, I made a thoughtless, unkind remark about the blue-jacketed members. The essence of my slur was that the people who join these organizations are snobby and do it for social status. Lise turned to me, unimpressed, and challenged my thinking in front of our small children. I mounted a weak defense but surrendered quickly. It was a hollow attempt. My comment was an illogical, unkind prejudice, deeply rooted in the insecurities of my childhood and my parent's money avoidance script.

While I think it is safe to say that my main money script today is vigilance—saving, investing, and protecting—I still wrestle with the less healthy scripts of my past. When my guard is down, the avoider and worshipper can both rear their ugly heads.

The Love of Money

SOME PEOPLE feel that too much interest in money is shallow or unspiritual and are quick to point out that the Bible says that "money is the root of all evil." This often misquoted verse actually says that "*the love of* money," not money itself, is the root of all kinds of evil.² Money is morally neutral. It can be a force for good or evil, arrogance or humility. It is the place that your money holds in your heart that counts.

Randy Alcorn, author of *Money, Possessions, and Eternity*, says there are 2,350 verses on the subject of money in the Bible, and that Jesus had more to say about money than Heaven or Hell.³ There is clearly nothing unspiritual about money, but it's still a loaded subject.

My friend Craig, who was raised in Thailand, understands this on a deeply personal level. When I asked him about his money script, he didn't hesitate when he responded with this childhood story:

> I grew up as a missionary kid. My family made a commitment to serve in Thailand and relied on the financial support of donors in our church. One hot, humid summer evening, I found myself on the stage of a Bible camp along with my parents and siblings. After a rousing series of old-time gospel hymns, we had been brought up onstage to share a brief recap of the work my parents did. I was also asked to say a few sentences in the Thai language, which I had learned overseas. I felt like a performing monkey. But the sideways glance from Dad told me this was not the time to take the higher ground.
>
> I had been engaged in this type of show-and-tell before, but what happened next made this July evening different. The host for the night moved to the microphone and gazed out at the crowd of comfortable Westerners. "Now people," he intoned, "this family needs

your help. And I know you want to bless them. Do I hear $3,000? How about $5,000?"

My family stood there, like lambs at an auction, as rich congregants stood up to the claps and praises of others. I looked out at the audience in utter humiliation. Holding back tears of shame, I vowed that when I grew up this would not happen to me again.

Early in my business career, I took unhealthy financial risks. Risks that set me and my family back. My quest to achieve "money status" and be seen as successful blinded me to financial realities. Thankfully my spouse, family, and good friends stuck with me through thick and thin.

To this day, I struggle with the entanglement of my self-worth with my net worth. It is hard to not want to take bigger business risks, but I seek out counsel of others who encourage me to be patient.

Self-Awareness Is Where Change Begins

KLONTZ AND Britt's money script research and predictive tools are based on 422 individual responses to a web survey conducted with the help of financial planners, coaches, and mental-health providers. The respondents were primarily middle age (forty-one to fifty), Caucasian (82%), and highly educated, with an average income of $65,000. This sampling is too small to be definitive when it comes to understanding everyone's thoughts and feelings on money. However, I do believe that the research has huge value. It has a language and thinking around it that is useful when trying to put words to our own deeper thoughts and feelings on this tender subject.

The Six Proven Principles for Financial Freedom, which you'll learn more about in the pages to come, are simple and should be easy to apply. The reasons we don't apply them are as complicated as we are. Taking time to contemplate the four money scripts—asking yourself what script you believe you most often follow, and why—can help you develop self-awareness, which is a critical first step in the process of short-circuiting unhealthy responses to irrational emotions that can rob you of the freedom and prosperity you deserve.

Take a few moments now and ask yourself the following four questions and summarize your thoughts and feelings in writing:

- Which of the four scripts—avoidance, worship, status, or vigilance—best describes my relationship with my finances? (If more than one, rank in order of dominance.)

- Where does this script come from? (A childhood experience, parents, inherited, etc.)

- Is this script working for or against me leading a happy, healthy financial life? How so?

- What positive changes can I make to improve my script today?

A SIMPLE SUMMARY

- How you feel about money is shaped by your family background.

- We all have irrational views and prejudices that hold us back.

- Being brutally honest with yourself about how you relate to money, and why, is critical.

- Money is morally neutral. It can be a force for good or evil, depending on whose hands it is in.

PART TWO

The Six Proven Principles for Financial Freedom

"Like the law of gravity, [these laws of money] are universal and unchanging."

GEORGE S. CLASON, *THE RICHEST MAN IN BABYLON*

4

Proven Principle #1: Save

———

You need money to make money. Which is why *saving 10% of all you earn is the first and most important of the Six Proven Principles.* It is the foundation on which all the other principles are based. If you get this rule right, your confidence and enthusiasm will grow with your bank balance and the rest will fall into place.

The day you start saving 10% of all you earn is a turning of the tide in your financial life, forever. By doing this, you are wresting control of your financial future away from the endless number of random demands, pressures, and impulsive desires of your everyday life. Either you manage your money, or your money will manage you and your family's life. The choice is yours.

I can appreciate how the uncompromising nature of this first principle might sound dramatic or unrealistic at first. I can assure you it isn't. Pretend for a moment that you earned 10% less than you do today, or that the government increased taxes by 10%. Would life as you know it end? Likely not. Most of us would grumble a bit, adjust to the new normal, and move on.

There can be no exceptions to this rule. Discretion is the enemy of order. Saving 10% of all you earn is the best way of defending you from yourself.

Whether it's losing weight, getting in shape, or saving money, we all tend to overestimate what we can achieve in one year and underestimate what we can achieve in twenty, thirty, or forty years. Every January, fitness facilities fill with enthusiastic new members huffing, puffing, and running their way into their new, fitter, trimmer selves. The super-fit regulars at the gym have seen it all before. They know the New Year's resolution crowds will be gone by Valentine's Day. They also know that the shape they are in is not the result of a few months' effort. True fitness is a marathon, not a sprint. A way of life, not an event.

In my previous life, I had some success at saving money. However, my next car, vacation, unexpected expense, or business idea usually ate it up... leaving the federal government waiting for their tax money and me scrambling. The problem I had was that my cost of living seemed to magically increase in direct proportion to my income. The more I made, the nicer my cars, clothes, and restaurant meals became. *Why not?* I thought. *I work hard. I deserve it.* Like most people, I had the process of saving backward. I was living on what I made and saving what was left over, instead of saving 10% and living on the balance.

A Metaphorical Bucket

THE BEST way to get started is to open a brand-new separate 10% savings account. Then, as you receive it, deposit
10% of every dollar you earn, from any and all sources, into
this account, without exception.

I remember Lise showing me our bank book with our
tiny balance after our first deposits. While a couple of
hundred dollars was small and hard to get excited about,
I do recall a flicker of hope sparked in me, knowing we
had begun. We had planted the seeds of our financial
future together. And with luck, they would grow. The most
important thing to remember is that when these funds are
deposited into your 10% account, they are no longer available to you, your family, your friends, or a creditor, for any
reason. This is *not* an emergency fund.

Once the money goes into this account, it never comes
out again, other than to invest wisely and safely for the day
that you are old and gray.

At first, your 10% account will be an actual bank
account. However, as your balance grows and you start
investing your savings in any one of a number of safe,
long-term investments (in other words, the stock market,
your own home, or income-producing real estate), your
10% account becomes a metaphorical bucket where your
savings compound. The returns on your 10% account
investments are always, and only, reinvested for your
future.

Desires Always Outpace Income

AS LISE and I struggled to get going again, it was tempting to look at the growing savings in our 10% account as a fall-back fund. But we knew our desires would always outpace our incomes, that making an exception and using it for any other purpose would be the beginning of the end. The 10% money was restricted. Gone! Unavailable to us forever, for anything other than investing wisely for our future.

This first and most important of all the principles is absolute—beyond negotiation.

A SIMPLE SUMMARY

- Saving 10% of all you earn is a foundational principle.

- If you don't manage your money, your money will manage you.

- As your bank balance grows, so too will your confidence and enthusiasm for saving.

- Your 10% account is a metaphorical bucket that represents the money you have saved and the investments you have made with those savings, such as your home, income properties, and stocks.

5

Proven Principle #2: Control

S I PULLED into the gas station near my home, my heart sank—and not because of the increased gas prices posted on the pump. My heart broke that day because of who I saw digging through the garbage cans looking for refundable bottles. The man and his wife appeared slim, healthy, and middle-class. Like the retirees we bump into running their dogs at the local off-leash park. The couple's embarrassment was made clear by their grim refusal to look anyone in the eye as they moved quickly from can to can. That encounter stuck with me. I wanted to know more. What had happened? What brought these people to this low point in their golden years?

I have a friend who volunteers at the local foodbank who says he was initially shocked by the number of average everyday seniors he meets who depend on its service. People you could never imagine needing a foodbank's support. I understand that the idea of controlling your expenses and developing the discipline required to live within your means is not exactly an exciting concept; it will require you to say no to certain people and opportunities today. What is exciting, however, is the thought of a better, brighter future: a life filled with options and opportunities, instead of regrets and debts.

If you save 10% of all you earn, control your expenses, and force yourself to live on the balance, you may experience an uncomfortable lifestyle adjustment. Our friends who ultimately failed, had debts, desires, or wants—which they confused with needs—that they felt they had to satisfy *before* they started saving for the future. They lacked the motivation and impulse control necessary to delay gratification in the interest of long-term gains. They failed to fully appreciate the almost immediate peace of mind you experience when you decide to take charge of your financial life and implement these simple ideas.

Today, more than ever before, we cannot rely on government pension plans to provide for us. Consider the money you save today a contribution into a self-imposed retirement fund for tomorrow. Your future depends on it.

Take a moment now before you read any further and visualize a new future free from empty bank accounts, unpaid bills, and the bondage of debt. Imagine a future that gives you the freedom to travel and pursue your passions, to care for the ones you love, and support the causes you care about. Hold these visions in your mind as you contemplate the adjustments you will need to make. Your perspective is everything. Our friends who gave up on these ideas saw them as sacrifices, instead of investments in a brighter future.

Needs and Wants

THE REALITY is that, no matter how much we earn, our cost of living will always grow in direct proportion to our incomes, *unless we protest otherwise.*

When you begin to look at controlling your expenses, clarify the difference between your needs and wants. We need food, shelter, clothing, and possibly a car. In choosing the type, size, or quality and quantity of these items, you encounter a wide range of possibilities, each with its own price tag. Thanks to online marketing, we are relentlessly pursued. Search engines and social media sites track our behavior and pop-up ads selling products and services related to our innocent searches follow us everywhere. In the battle for financial control of your life, reject these marketing messages with the disdain they deserve and choose cost-efficient ways of addressing your true needs in a financially intelligent way. Embrace the idea of short-term sacrifice for long-term gain. Remember that less is ultimately more, that delaying gratification of a desire today can pay huge dividends tomorrow.

Why We Do What We Do

WHEN IT comes to controlling your expenses, it is important to understand why you make the decisions you make. It takes courage to lean into and dwell upon the mistakes that have cost you the most in the past. But this introspection plays a critical role in the development of the self-awareness you need to be successful.

My impulsive decision to buy a car when I was twenty-two is a personal example. I had made the mistake of dropping into a GM dealership to "have a look" and drove a new sports car off the lot three hours later. I will never forget the range of emotions I felt as I paced around the shiny new collector's edition Corvette. The powerful 350-cubic-inch engine and the smell of the soft, supple leather interior left me weak in the knees. My heart beat quickly and the hair on the back of my neck stood up. Every fiber of my twenty-two-year-old being wanted to possess that automobile. When I finally summoned the courage to ask, "How much?" I was done. The payments on my new $32,000 car were $687 per month. I drove it home that afternoon, smiling from ear to ear. I could not believe my good fortune.

One year later, when things weren't going as well, I sold my dream car. My $10,000 down payment and the twelve monthly payments of $687 were lost. Buying and financing a $32,000 vehicle at the age of twenty-two made no financial sense whatsoever. So, what happened? What caused this temporary insanity and departure from reality?

Travis Bradberry and Jean Greaves, coauthors of *Emotional Intelligence 2.0*, believe our brains are hardwired to give our emotions the upper hand. Apparently, everything we see, smell, hear, taste, or touch travels through our bodies in the form of electric signals. These signals pass from cell to cell until they reach and enter our brains at its base, near the spinal cord. Then they travel up to our frontal lobe, where rational, logical thinking takes place. The challenge is that along the way these sense perceptions pass through the limbic system, where emotions are produced. This journey ensures that we experience life emotionally before reason kicks into gear. Bradberry and Greaves suggest that the communication between the emotional and rational parts of the brain is the physical source of emotional intelligence.[1]

As a young man of twenty-two, the rational and emotional sides of my brain were not fully aware of each other's existence. Painful thoughts and feelings on subjects such as unpaid income taxes were always pushed aside in favor of more positive thoughts and feelings like buying a new Corvette or the party on the weekend. My emotions often had the upper hand.

We are emotional beings. When it comes to controlling our expenses, we all have our own unique passions, fears, interests, and desires that can trigger irrational feelings. These emotions often move quickly into actions we regret later. Taking time to review your past mistakes gives you a deeper understanding of hidden emotional drivers that you can defend against in the future.

In the interest of protecting you from yourself, here are some questions you might ask. Take some time thinking about them and write down your answers.

- What financial decisions have I made in the past that I regret today?
- How can I make sure I do not repeat them?
- What areas of my life are most vulnerable to unhealthy spending behavior?
- What are some creative, cost-effective ways to enjoy my wants today without sacrificing my financial tomorrow?

A New Way of Life

AFTER DECLARING bankruptcy and reading *The Richest Man in Babylon*, I spent many quiet hours looking at where I went wrong. The sting of my failures was humbling and painful. But it deepened my resolve to not repeat them again.

In an effort to control our expenses and save more, one of the first big changes Lise and I made were the types of cars we drove. The fancy sports cars I had financed and couldn't afford were replaced by older American cars that I bought for $1,000 or $2,000 cash. I recall rattling home from work one evening in one of the most beat-up cars we had ever owned. A large hole in the muffler made it sound like a Sherman tank. As I stopped at an intersection, the muffler backfired, as it usually did, sending a large cloud of blue smoke into the air. Aware of the attention I might be attracting from fellow motorists, I casually glanced to my left and caught two young men, sitting in a late-model sports car, laughing at me and my beater.

In my previous life, I would have flushed with anger and given them the one-finger salute. However, Lise and I were three years into our new life and things were going well. I was making great money. We had just moved into our first home. Our bills were paid, our 10% savings account was growing, and Lise was pregnant for the first time. We could have afforded a nicer car and still saved and invested, but I took pride in my $1,000 special. The progress we were making, and the peace of mind that this new life brought, meant more to me than any car. We were finding this financially intelligent life addictive, and we wanted more.

So, when the light turned green, I hit the gas and left my audience behind in a puff of smoke. I had a big grin on my face that said, "We have a plan. Our dreams are coming true, slowly but surely, one day at a time."

As your 10% account grows, you will find the temporary pleasure you took in spending replaced by a desire to find new and better ways to save more. Start carefully looking at your spending habits. As you examine your expenses, hold one question in your mind: is this a need or a want? Make a list. Once you have separated the two, take time to quietly review and reflect.

- Am I getting full value for every dollar I spend?
- Are there more cost-effective ways of meeting my needs?

YOLO

IT'S TRUE that you only live once, and you want to make the most of it. You want to pursue your passions with all your heart. You may want to see the world and explore new cultures and experiences. To volunteer. Or try a new career that doesn't pay a living wage. Like me being a writer.

All of these are admirable objectives. But they all require time, money, and—unless you are rich or win the lottery—some sacrifice. None of them is a God-given right. They are experiences and opportunities that are made richer when you *earn* the right to enjoy them. Controlling your expenses and living a financially intelligent life today will give you the freedom you need to explore your personal passions tomorrow.

Get Out and Stay Out of Debt

COMPOUNDING IS one of the greatest forces of financial nature there is. However, it works both ways: it works for you when you save and it works against you when you carry personal debt. If you are reading this and are currently buried in an avalanche of personal debt, you are likely asking yourself how you can in good conscience save 10% of all you earn and still meet your obligations. The short answer is it won't be easy, but it can be done.

The better question is: what will my financial future look like if I don't start saving now?

You may have to ask creditors to extend payment terms longer than you originally agreed upon. This is not an unusual request. Lenders are often receptive to restructuring a payment plan when they know the alternative is non-payment. Getting back on your feet financially is in everyone's best interest.

A SIMPLE SUMMARY

- Your cost of living will always increase in direct proportion to your income—unless you protest otherwise.

- You need to distinguish between needs and wants and look for the most cost-effective ways of meeting your needs.

- As your bank balance grows, the temporary pleasure you used to take in spending will be replaced with a desire to find new and better ways to save more money.

- Controlling your expenses today is a short-term sacrifice you can make for a better tomorrow.

6

Proven Principle #3: Multiply

————

MONEY NEVER SLEEPS. It's a tireless laborer, working twenty-four hours a day, seven days a week. It never comes in late or asks for a break, a raise, or a vacation. The only thing your money needs from you is profitable employment.

At a rate of 7% per year, a conservative long-term rate of return in the stock market, your money doubles every ten years. Compounding investment returns is the most awesome force of financial nature there is. Those who understand it, earn it. Those who don't, pay it.

One of the least-appreciated secrets of wealth creation is money's ability to duplicate itself. So, to make sure you fully understand the radical, life-changing implications of this eighth wonder of the world, I am going to ask you to suspend reality for a moment and travel with me to an alternative universe. In this new world, we don't click, tap, or scan our way through the day. The currency here is ping-pong balls. But these are not just any ping-pong balls.

They are magical, golden ping-pong balls that reproduce themselves at a rate of 7% per year when you save them.

So, if you earn 60,000 ping-pong balls a year, and save 10%, or 500 balls a month, you will have 6,000 golden ping-pong balls in storage containers in your basement rec room at the end of your first year of saving. If you are financially intelligent, earn the same amount, and stick to that plan for a decade, at the end of the tenth year, you will have saved 60,000 balls. But because these ping-pong balls magically reproduce at a compound rate of 7% a year, you instead have over 85,000 golden ping-pong balls—stacked from floor to ceiling in both your basement rec room and your furnace room. Storage space is becoming a major issue, but it's a nice problem to have.

If you have the discipline to stick to the plan and save 500 balls a month, without spending any of the balls:

- After twenty years, the 120,000 balls you saved will have grown to over 250,000.

- After thirty years, the 180,000 balls you saved will have grown to over 580,000.

- After forty years, the 240,000 balls you saved will have grown to over *1.2 million golden ping-pong balls*.

You are a ping-pong ball millionaire!

Notice how the rate accelerates over the years? When it comes to compounding, time is your friend. After twenty years, the number of ping-pong balls has a little more than doubled. However, in the fourth decade, the 240,000 balls that you have saved (6,000 balls per year for forty years) will have grown to 1.2 million. Five times more than you placed in storage.

Congratulations! You now have a forty-five-foot shipping container in your backyard, filled from top to bottom with 1.2 million golden ping-pong balls, reproducing themselves at a rate of 7% per year. This gives you 91,000 balls a year to live on. Far more than you earned at your day job. By this time, you have paid off your home and are ready to retire. To celebrate, you have just booked a first-class trip around the world.

The forty-five-foot shipping container in your backyard is as long as your property is wide. It is nine-and-a-half feet high and eight feet wide. It has a 1.4 million ball capacity, if you save much more, you will be shopping for another container. All of this has been accomplished by living within your means and saving only 500 ping-pong balls a month.

Unfortunately, retirement hasn't gone quite as well for your best friends and next-door neighbors, Fred and Betty Smith. You live in identical homes that you bought from the same developer thirty years ago. Coincidentally, they are the same age and have always had the same household income as you have.

The Smiths have always led active lives, motorcycling and golfing in the summer, skiing and traveling in the winter. They went to the same all-inclusive resort in Mexico for years. The life of every party, they have matching T-shirts with #YOLO and a sombrero on the front and BEACH PARTY CABO on the back.

The Smiths have slowed down a lot lately. Their health is fine, but they are struggling financially. They tried saving over the years, but something more important always came up. There are no ping-pong balls in their cupboards or their closets, and only an echo in their empty basement. The Smiths never liked talking about ping-pong balls or investing; they found the subjects boring and shallow.

Unfortunately, the pension plans they have been depending on only pay half of what they earned when they were working. To make matters worse, they had refinanced their home to pay off high-interest credit card debt. Their newly reduced retirement income won't cover their mortgage payments, so they are selling and moving into their daughter's basement suite. The Smiths have no ping-pong balls and nowhere else to go.

Live for Today but Plan for Tomorrow

AS THE Smiths were always quick to point out, it is important to live for today. However, it is equally important to plan for tomorrow. Chances are, like the Smiths, you will be old and gray one day and want to travel the world. You may want to help your children or grandchildren with their education or first home or, better yet, spend more time and money supporting the causes you care about.

When making money multiply, always remember that you are playing the long game. Seeking wisdom and counsel is important but make the final investment decisions yourself. Knowledge is power and delegating this responsibility to a money manager is an investment in their education, instead of your own.

If you are intimidated by this idea, don't worry. In Part Three, Financially Intelligent Investing, you will discover powerful proven strategies that work perfectly for the know-nothing investor. In my experience, the novice with a disciplined long-term approach will outperform the professional every time.

A SIMPLE SUMMARY

- At 7% per year, your money doubles every ten years.

- When it comes to making money with money, time is your friend.

- You cannot retire comfortably on government pension plans alone. Live for today, but plan for tomorrow.

7

Proven Principle #4: Protect

—————

THERE ARE VERY few things in life that I hate more than being taken advantage of. When that happens, like anyone else, I get to choose how I respond. I can get lost in the emotion of the experience and blame the dishonest perpetrator. Or I can look hard at my role in the affair and ask myself what I did that allowed me to be taken advantage of in the first place. By leaning into these experiences and scratching beneath the surface of the narrative that I use to explain my behavior to myself, I am forced to confront aspects of my character that I would sometimes rather ignore; so, it hurts. However, this process plays a critical role in the development of the self-awareness I need to be a better investor.

Arkad, the richest man in Babylon, talks about the first investment he made with his friend, a bricklayer. Lured by the promise of huge profits, he invested one year of hard-earned savings in a diamond buying scheme. Predictably, his bricklaying buddy came back from his trip with a bag full of worthless glass. The moral of this story is don't trust a bricklayer to buy diamonds. Unfortunately, that is exactly what I did when I invested in a large condominium development project in 2005.

I was introduced to this opportunity by a business associate who was helping the developer, a retired professional athlete, raise money. My first meeting with the developer was over lunch with one of his famous friends, who was also his largest partner. I soon discovered that most of the investors were professional athletes.

A few years later, when the project went into receivership, it was discovered that this affable, charismatic real estate developer was actually a fraudster who had been stealing money from the company. He had been flying around in private jets with friends and former teammates while defrauding investors on a grand scale. The boldness of his dishonesty, which came to light in an audit after the banks took control, was staggering.

In retrospect, my decision to invest in this project was not made from a rational point of view. I knew nothing about the true state of the financial affairs of the company, and nothing about the development business. I put blind trust in an inexperienced retired athlete running a privately owned development company; he had control over all decisions *and the checkbook*.

After the smoke had cleared and the sting of my poor decision-making subsided, I began looking closer at the fiasco and asking myself why I had gotten involved and allowed myself to be taken advantage of. The short answer is *pride*. The cachet of investing with a bunch of famous athletes was hard to resist. I was blinded by my desire to be a part of something "special," and I paid the price. My total return on that investment was a baseball hat and a bruised ego. I felt foolish and ashamed.

Never Lose Money

WHEN I had finally turned the corner financially and had money to invest beyond my real estate portfolio, I didn't know I was operating under the same false assumption that many newly minted entrepreneurs do regarding their investment prowess. Running a successful business requires a different set of skills than managing money does. Being a successful entrepreneur requires a high level of self-confidence, a hubris that allows you to believe the unbelievable and succeed where others might fail. This optimism and inflated sense of self got in my way.

Legendary investor Warren Buffett has two main rules: "1. Don't lose money. 2. Don't forget the first rule."[1] These may sound trite, but do not dismiss them as witty wisdom. Buffett's success as the greatest investor in the world has been built on these rules. Stuffing your savings into a mattress for ten years is far better than losing money on a bad investment. At least when you return to your mattress, your savings are still there.

Successful Investing Is a Marathon, Not a Sprint

I HAD an elderly neighbor named Harry who passed away at the age of ninety. He was a gregarious, colorful man, always ready with an interesting story from his past.

Lise recalls him answering the door with a thick wad of $100 bills sticking out of his breast-pocket on more than one occasion. Concerned for his safety, she would encourage him to be more discreet. He always waved this warning off with a chuckle and stories of how well he had just done at the casino—apparently he always won. When I saw Harry's daughter at a neighborhood gathering recently, I commented on her father's good luck. When I did, she didn't smile. She explained that his gambling had become a serious problem in his declining years.

Most investors are far too cavalier in their investing approach. They play the stock market like Harry played a slot machine—celebrating wins and pretending their losses don't exist. Successful investing is a marathon, not a sprint. A way of life, not an event. If you do the right things today, tomorrow will take care of itself.

As a new investor, you must have your antenna up and be tuned in to the ever-changing world around you. In the process, new and exciting ways to invest will surface. When this happens, remember that risking your capital by chasing higher returns is the biggest mistake most investors make. Risk and return are inseparably linked. We don't get one without the other. Knowledge and experience can reduce risk, but rely on *your* knowledge and experience, not someone else's.

When I look back at poor investment decisions I have made over the years, it's easy to see where I went wrong. As a salesman and entrepreneur, I had learned to think positively. To take chances and believe in the unbelievable to survive. So, when someone presents a new investment opportunity to me, I can get excited. My limbic system starts firing and my emotions take control. I want to believe for my fellow entrepreneur; it's in my nature. However, in the process, I can get swept up in the excitement of the moment and end up buying worthless glass, or shares in condo projects from athletes, instead of diamonds.

Thankfully, today I know myself well enough to know that I can be impulsive. That I shouldn't make financial decisions on the spot. So, no matter how exciting something sounds, I listen politely with an open mind but never commit to anything immediately. Instead I go home and sleep on it.

The next morning the salesman in me refers the matter to my alter ego, the grumpy accountant. He operates almost exclusively from the rational/logical part of my brain. After a cursory review of the matter, he usually shakes his head, wonders what the salesman was thinking, and gives the idea a quick thumbs-down. My accountant is not a people pleaser. He can't afford to be.

If It Sounds Too Good to Be True...

WHEN YOUR brother-in-law goes on and on at Thanksgiving dinner about a new investment opportunity with great returns and no risk, do not be fooled. It may be a Ponzi scheme.

A Ponzi scheme is the financial equivalent of musical chairs. It uses money raised from new investors to pay old investors returns on an investment that does not exist.

Fraudsters raise this money by promoting complex investment strategies that promise irresistible returns.

Ponzi schemes pop up regularly, targeting large and small investors alike. They are always surrounded by a lot of hype and encourage new participants to share their "special" opportunity with friends and relatives. Everyone is always happy and excited until the music stops when the promoters run out of new players for their game.

The highest profile example of this in recent years is the Ponzi scheme run by former Wall Street financier Bernard Madoff. Over two decades, he successfully swindled more than $17 billion from unsuspecting, supposedly sophisticated investors and money managers. He did this by leveraging his track record as a successful Wall Street securities dealer and former chairman of NASDAQ, one of the largest stock exchanges in the world. At the age of seventy-one, he was handed a 150-year sentence for his crimes and will spend the balance of his life behind bars.

What made Madoff's scheme unique is that the victims were mostly high net worth individuals who were members of New York's high society and charitable foundations. Many hedge funds and money managers liked the high returns so much that they created feeder funds to funnel billions of dollars of their client's money into Madoff's Ponzi scheme. Harry Markopolos, a financial analyst and portfolio manager who worked for Rampart Investment Management in Boston, was asked by his employers in 2001 to design an investment product that would replicate Madoff's returns. After only four hours of trying, and failing, to replicate Madoff's purported strategy, Markopolos concluded that it was a mathematical impossibility, that it had to be a Ponzi scheme.

Alarmed by what he was seeing, Markopolos wrote three consecutive letters to the Securities and Exchange Commission outlining his concerns in detail. Apparently, some lame inquiries were made by the SEC, but no substantive action was taken. At that time, Madoff managed assets of between $3 and $6 billion, making it the largest hedge fund in the world.

It wasn't until seven years later, in 2008, during the sudden and dramatic downturn in the stock market, caused by the subprime mortgage crises, that the fraud was revealed.[2] As Buffett is often quoted, "When the tide goes out, you get to see who has been swimming naked."

One of the saddest parts of this whole tale is what it says about the highly paid money managers running these feeder funds. The size and consistency of the returns that Madoff paid made no sense. What took Harry Markopolos only *four hours* to discover supposedly went undetected by Wall Street's best and brightest for years. They were blinded by greed and either complicit or reckless in the extreme. Both represent a total dereliction of duty.

In the final analysis, it was Madoff's veneer of respectability as a legitimate securities dealer, socialite, and prominent member of the Jewish community in New York City that made him so successful. Fraudulently exploiting relationships based on religious affiliations, culture, or ethnicity is known as *affinity fraud*. It is a popular tactic used by swindlers of all stripes who ingratiate themselves into churches and other spiritual communities.

Never forget that if something sounds too good to be true, it is. When someone approaches you with a "once in a lifetime" opportunity, with great returns and little risk, they are lying or being deceived. In either case, don't waste your time debating. The fast-talking gregarious promoter will have smooth answers to all your questions.

Think twice, act once, and invest only in areas you understand and can control.

A SIMPLE SUMMARY

- You will make mistakes. Everyone does.

- Take responsibility for your mistakes and learn from them.

- Risk and reward are inseparably linked.

- Never commit to anything immediately. Sleep on it.

- Most con artists are friendly and smart. If it sounds too good to be true, it is.

8

Proven Principle #5: Own

ONCE A YEAR, my family and I make our way down to Tijuana, Mexico, and spend two days in the dusty hills with fifteen other volunteer-donors building a home for a poor family. The families we build for have been selected by Youth With A Mission's Homes of Hope, a volunteer Christian organization that has built thousands of homes for those in need over the years.

Every year we build a home is the same. When we arrive on the job site Saturday morning, a 400-square-foot concrete slab has already been poured. Next to this pad is the family's current home: a collection of scrap lumber, corrugated metal, and worn-out dirty tarps thrown together over a damp dirt floor in an effort to keep out the elements. The 800-square-foot lot that the home sits on was bought by the family from a local developer for $4,000. Banks don't lend to the poor, so the seller usually finances the purchase with a $400 down payment, which the buyer has taken years to save.

After two days of frenzied effort, we are sunburnt, covered in paint, tired, and sore. But thanks to the help and leadership of the Homes of Hope volunteer staff, a new home with sliding windows, a locking front door, and a weather-proof asphalt shingle roof has been built and furnished. By this time, we also have taken the mother grocery shopping, stocking the family's cupboards and fridge, and bought the kids a few toys.

The closing ceremony is always the same. We stand in a circle, taking turns sharing a word of blessing and encouragement for the family. When the mother finally speaks, the tears streaming down her face, and our faces too, the impact of what has taken place that weekend sinks in: a family's life has been transformed, forever, by a home. A home of hope.

HOMEOWNERSHIP IS the cornerstone of most people's retirement savings plan. I cannot count the number of financially unsophisticated retirees I have met over the years who have said things like, "We don't know anything about money or the stock market. We bought our home when we were married and paid it off because our parents said we should. If we hadn't, we would be broke today."

Owning your home has two features that make it a unique and powerful investment. The first is pride of ownership. Whether you live in Tijuana or Toledo, the desire to own a home, a place to call your own, resides deep in the hearts and souls of most people. Homeownership is about family, community, and legacy. It transcends dollars and cents and says, "We belong."

The second feature that makes homeownership an exceptional investment is leverage. With a relatively small down payment, you can "lever" the bank's money to own a large asset that will go up in value over time.

Thirty years ago, we bought our first home, a town-house, for $125,000 with a $12,500 (10%) down payment. Out of interest, I went online recently to see what a town-home in our old complex sells for today. Thirty years later, the exact same type of unit we bought for $125,000 is selling for $560,000. If all we had ever done was live in that townhouse, our $12,500 down payment would be worth $560,000 today (an average annual return of 13.5%).

If we had taken that same $12,500 and invested in government bonds at 3% per year, after thirty years we would have $30,000 in bonds—instead of a clear title townhouse worth $560,000.

That is the magic of homeownership, and *leverage*.

WELL-SELECTED HOMEOWNERSHIP is one of the best long-term investments the average person can make. It is a hedge against inflation and a form of forced savings. Children of homeowners also perform better at school. Moving less often creates a more stable home environment, which positively affects academic performance. A study published by the *Real Estate Economics* journal found that children of homeowners performed 9% better in math and 7% better in reading than children of non-homeowners.[1]

There is something very comforting and reassuring about living in a clear title home when you are about to retire. Few people would argue this point. However, I do bump into the odd dissenter now and then. They are almost always money managers who say that homeownership doesn't, in their parlance, "pencil out." They are convinced that the money used for a down payment would get better returns elsewhere.

Some less-than-scrupulous financial planners use this same argument to convince unsophisticated consumers to sell or borrow against their homes to invest with them. The returns these salespeople promote may look good on paper, but without a crystal ball, no one can predict the future.

Of course, buying a home is a personal decision, and there are exceptions to all rules. It may not be realistic for everyone. For example, if you are forced to move often because of your work or another circumstance, you may have to sell at the wrong time. The value of real estate, like any other asset, goes up and down. So, make your buying decision thoughtfully. Ask yourself if you would be comfortable living in the home for the next ten years, a safe holding period, if you had to.

You may also live in one of the many major cities in the world where, thanks to low interest rates, home prices have skyrocketed in value. Prices in these markets have forced motivated buyers to be creative.

- Adult children are partnering with parents or siblings on homes with in-law accommodations.

- Parents with means are bequeathing inheritances early, gifting or lending down payments to their kids.

- Some people simply move to another city where real estate prices are affordable. This sacrifice allows them to achieve their dream of homeownership sooner rather than later.

A SIMPLE SUMMARY

- Owning a home is the cornerstone of most people's retirement savings plans.

- A home is the only investment the average person can borrow against.

- Leverage supercharges investment returns.

- Owning your own home is safer than trusting someone else to manage your money.

9

Proven Principle #6: Increase

WORKING HARD IS admirable, rewarding, and necessary. Particularly when you are starting out in life. However, working *smart* is what counts the most when trying to get ahead in life. *Earning more* is always better than *working more*, so make a habit of studying those around you who are being more productive. Ask yourself, What are they doing that I can do? How did they get where they are? Be a lifelong learner. If you do *exactly* what they did, you will get the same results.

If you are not currently in your dream job, do not be discouraged or distracted by the short-sighted, negative people around you. No matter what you do for a living, always go the extra mile. Look at your work as a necessary next step, a transition point to bigger and better things.

That is exactly what I did when, at the age of twenty, I took a job as a commission-only telemarketer, the lowest rung on the sales-job ladder. This particular company hired almost anyone who walked through the door. We joked that there was only one test a new salesperson had to pass. A mirror was placed in front of their face and if fog appeared, they were hired. Needless to say, the cast of characters I worked elbow to elbow with in these smoke-filled rooms was colorful. Many viewed their work as a necessary evil that had to be endured—and their paychecks reflected those attitudes.

Being ambitious, I gave this low-level job all that I had. The official starting time was 9 a.m. However, I always showed up at 7:45 a.m., made a cup of coffee, got myself organized, and, like clockwork, picked up the phone at exactly 8 a.m.—one full hour before many of my reluctant coworkers showed up.

Most of the people I worked with dismissed the value of starting early, saying that businesses weren't open yet. My friends were mostly right; I spoke to a lot of answering services in that first hour. However, I also discovered that some business owners liked getting in early to get a jump on their day. Undefended by the receptionists who would screen me out during the day, they picked up the phone themselves—giving me an opportunity I never would have had otherwise.

That first hour in the morning gave me a huge advantage in sales and momentum. I was always one of the top salespeople. Predictably, my enthusiasm and work ethic garnered snide remarks and gossip, but I could care less; my coworkers weren't paying my rent.

Not surprisingly, my hard work and discipline were quickly noticed by management and in a matter of months I was promoted to sales manager, supervising fifty telemarketers. I was now earning a generous commission on my friends' sales. My coworkers saw a lousy job. I saw opportunity.

RAAGINI, OR Ra, and his wife Botum, or Bo, also have a story that exemplifies this principle perfectly. They met in a refugee camp on the Thai side of the Cambodian border. They had fled for their lives just ahead of Pol Pot and his brutal Khmer Rouge regime; 1,500,000 of their fellow Cambodians, including friends and relatives, were not as lucky. Bo and Ra were married in the camp that they languished in for years while they searched desperately for a Western nation that would grant them asylum. I am proud to say that Canada eventually took them in.

I met Ra and Bo for the first time as tenants of a commercial property we own. I don't meet most applicants; we pay property managers well to handle these negotiations. However, when I received their offer to lease and heard their story, I felt I had to meet them.

They were in the process of buying a business from one of our existing tenants and had to negotiate a new lease with us, the landlord. The tenant whose business they were purchasing was regularly behind on his rent, so we were happy at the prospect of new tenants. What I found so exceptional about Ra and Bo's offer was the financial statement attached to it. They had $250,000 in a savings account and owned a home with $300,000 in equity.

When I finally met this humble couple and heard their story, I was deeply touched. They had come to Canada thirty years earlier as penniless refugees and settled in a small town. Bo found a minimum wage job at a coffee shop, where she stayed for twenty-five years. Ra secured full-time employment on the assembly line at a local factory and took a part-time job in the kitchen of a Vietnamese restaurant. He kept both jobs for twenty-five years.

Neither Ra nor Bo have a strong command of the English language or much in the way of formal education. Their options were limited but they did the best they could with what they had. Ra *increased his ability to earn* by taking a part-time job in a restaurant. They lived well within their means and saved as much as they could to buy a house, and then a small business that employs their whole family—their dream come true.

A SIMPLE SUMMARY

- Be enthusiastic. Always go the extra mile. It gives you a huge edge.

- Don't be discouraged by short-sighted, negative people around you.

- Earning more is better than working more.

- Be a lifelong learner.

PART THREE

Financially
Intelligent
Investing

"There are two times in a man's life

when he should not speculate:

when he can't afford it, and when he can."

MARK TWAIN, *FOLLOWING THE EQUATOR*

10

Are You Speculating
or Investing?

AT THE HEIGHT of the digital gold rush of the 1990s, my friend Bensen made the pilgrimage to Wall Street, the mecca of capitalism, to learn the art of day-trading. Day traders buy and sell a stock in minutes or hours. Never holding a position overnight, they often trade on margin, which is borrowed money, and make their bets based on trading volume and momentum, instead of value.

During his time there, the NASDAQ rose 400%, and he made millions.

The music stopped in 2002 when the dot-com boom went bust and the market fell by 80%. Thankfully, Bensen saw it coming and was disciplined enough to quit while he was ahead. Greed got the better of most of his friends, who kept rolling the dice, and they were forced to give their profits back.

If you had asked me then what Bensen did for a living, I would have said, "He is a full-time *investor* who day-trades technology stocks." Of course, nothing was further from the truth. Day-trading is a form of *speculation*, not investing. Unfortunately, there is no widespread consensus on the definition of these two terms. Many investors wander aimlessly between the two worlds, losing money as they go.

When I began expanding my investment horizons, I lost money in a number of creative ways, including business start-ups, junior stocks, limited partnerships, private equity, and mezzanine financing funds. I didn't realize it then, but I was *speculating*—not *investing*. The only people making any money on most of these deals were the people promoting them.

I eventually grew tired of losing money on broken promises and bad advice. Today I stick to income-producing real estate and blue-chip, dividend-paying, publicly traded equities. Assets with a long, strong, discernable track record of value and performance. Our investment policy is *simple*: quality people and quality assets.

Are you *investing* or *speculating*? Make sure you know the difference.

Four Reasons Why Real Estate Is a Great Investment

THE KIND-HEARTED Italian families that impressed me as an eighteen-year-old realtor, Franco's father, and millions of other unsophisticated investors all invest in income-producing real estate for the same four main reasons:

1   It's an asset that most people can understand, evaluate, and control.

2   It's a great hedge against inflation; as the cost of living goes up, real estate values go up with it.

3   It offers leverage. The ability to borrow money against a property allows you to make money with the bank's money.

4   It offers the intangible but very real pride of ownership, which no other investment product has.

The first income-producing property we purchased with our 10% account savings was a beat-up, old, three-bedroom rancher in the Flats, a lower-income neighborhood in our community. We were drawn to the property by the motivated seller's newspaper ad offering a $4,000 down payment and $79,000 price tag. On the surface, this little house sounded like an accident waiting to happen. But we were excited and prepared for the challenge.

We ended up owning that rental house for twenty years. It more than doubled in value in that time. We turned our first $4,000 investment into $189,000—an annualized rate of return of 21.5%.

Stay Close to Home

WHEN INVESTING in rental properties, it is a good idea to stay close to home. Look for properties you will drive by on the way to work or the grocery store. Franco's father bought five duplexes all within the same two-block radius so that he and his boys could stay on top of maintenance and tenant issues. Franco and his brothers didn't need a car or truck: they just pushed the lawnmower or carried their shovels and rakes from house to house.

Many investors, including myself, are often lured out of the neighborhoods they know best by the promise of higher returns, only to be disappointed later. A rental property we bought five years after buying our little home in the Flats is a perfect example. Lise and I thought we had found a great deal in a small community about a four-hour drive away from our home. It was an old duplex with an additional unauthorized one-bedroom suite in the basement. The $300 per month in positive cash flow looked great on paper, but the reality was different.

After closing on the property, circumstances went from bad to worse quickly. First, I received a letter from the city zoning department that our basement suite was unauthorized and that we had to stop renting it. Also, because I was an absentee owner, I had to rely on a professional property management company that was not very professional. For the main floor suite, they found us a tenant who stopped paying rent after the first month. After repeated notices and threats, we had to begin the legal process of eviction. It took eight months of notices and legal proceedings to get the tenant out. Two years after buying it, we sold the property for $20,000 less than we paid for it.

If I had lived in the community and not rushed into buying the duplex, I may have known that the city would not turn a blind eye to the unauthorized basement suite. I would also have been there to screen applicants, likely saving myself from my "tenant from hell" experience. Of course, there would have been no guarantee of the reliability of a tenant I picked personally either. But at least I would have been there to manage the property when there was a problem. Instead, I was forced to depend on an unmotivated, incompetent property manager.

In-Law or Basement Suites

WHEN STARTING out as an investor, the size and type of property you can invest in will be limited by the size of mortgage you qualify for and the amount of your down payment. One way many new investors ease their way into income property ownership is by buying a home with rental income potential. A basement suite or a suite over a detached garage can provide you with income to acquire a larger asset than you are able to afford on your own.

Renting a suite to tenants in your primary residence is a perfect example of a short-term sacrifice for a long-term gain. Of course, tenants have pluses and minuses. On the plus side, managing the property and the tenant will be easy, since you live on-site. The minus is that you live on-site. After we sold our first townhome, we bought an older single-family home with a basement suite that we rented out to a young doctor and his wife. A nice couple who paid their rent on time, they were building their own home and needed a place for a year. However, we discovered quickly that the doctor's wife had a bad temper. Every few weeks or so, she could be heard ranting and raving at the poor doctor. I guess the stress of new home construction was getting to her. When they eventually moved out, we decided we didn't need the income, or noise, so the suite became my home office.

Tenant Selection

THE INCOME stream from your rental properties will only be as dependable as your tenant, which is why smart landlords screen their tenants carefully. Always confirm the applicant's credit history and landlord references. A potential tenant's credit report, which can be accessed online for a nominal fee, is the most objective data a landlord can have. If an applicant has a history of paying bills late, or not at all, they will have no qualms about treating you the same way. Be careful not to be swayed by glib excuses from blame-shifters. Some people are brilliant at making unsuspecting landlords feel guilty for not "helping" them. Recognize these dishonest attempts at manipulation for what they are. Be clear about your expectations and stick to your guns in a firm but friendly way. And don't rely entirely on references; there is no way to confirm their objectivity. The previous landlord may want to move a bad tenant along or have a personal relationship that affects their opinion.

Quality properties attract quality people. If you want great tenants with great credit histories, you have to offer a quality, competitive product. That doesn't mean that your rental property needs custom finishes. But it should be well maintained, clean, and in good functional order.

Mortgage Financing

WHEN INVESTING in real estate, whether it is your own home or an income property, and using leverage, you will need financing. When determining the size of mortgage you qualify for, lenders will consider your household income, the size of your down payment, and your credit rating.

Before negotiating the purchase of a property, it is wise to determine the size of mortgage you can comfortably carry. Your bank, or a mortgage broker who represents multiple lenders, can walk you through the prequalifying process, at no cost. Being armed with this information in advance will help you negotiate with confidence.

When considering real estate, which is an active rather than passive investment, it is important to ask yourself a few questions:

- Is real estate a wise investment for me at this stage of my life, given my income, career, temperament, and lifestyle?

- If so, what type of real estate should I start with? My own home, a home with a rental suite, or an income property?

- How large of a mortgage will I qualify for and be able to comfortably carry?

- What size of down payment do I require—including legal fees, taxes, and adjustments?

A SIMPLE SUMMARY

- Income-producing real estate is a great hedge against inflation.

- Do not be lured away from your own neighborhood by the promise of higher returns. Buy properties you can manage yourself.

- Quality properties attract quality tenants.

- Choose tenants carefully. Bad tenants are easier to get than they are to get rid of.

- Getting prequalified for a mortgage will help you to negotiate with confidence.

11

Make the Market
Your Friend

———

ALWAYS LIKED INVESTING in real estate because I could feel it and touch it. I could bring my entrepreneurial skills, talents, and street smarts to the day-to-day operation of a property with no risk that I'd wake up one morning and discover the property had vanished, like some companies do.

However, owning and managing rental properties is an active, not a passive, investment. Dealing with realtors, tenants, and the maintenance of the properties requires an investment of time and emotional energy. For a variety of reasons—career, lifestyle, or personality—this type of investing is not a fit for everyone. If that is your case, the next most obvious place to start making your money multiply safely over the long term is the stock market.

If you have no experience or training in this area, it can be an intimidating subject to think about, at first. The financial services industry has a language all its own—

shorts, longs, bears and bulls, futures and commodities. The list is long. Add to this the nonstop financial news cycle with talking heads droning on and on, debating the impact of every political and economic event. It's enough to make anyone's head spin, which is why most novice investors wave the white flag and surrender their financial futures to a professional money manager.

I believe that *most* financial advisors are good and basically honest people who believe they are operating in the best interests of their clients. Unfortunately, the financial industry's business model is fundamentally flawed. Professional advisors are salespeople. They are paid commissions and fees on the products they sell by the institutions they represent. The more you invest, and the more frequently you trade, the more money your advisor makes, even if you don't see a return. No matter how good or honest they are, the business model they operate in makes it impossible for them to be entirely objective. I ignored the stock market for the first fifteen years of my investing career for these very reasons. However, I had to adjust my strategy when I sold a business and found myself with more capital to invest than my real estate portfolio could absorb. I needed to diversify.

After a couple of unhappy experiences with money managers, it became clear that I would have to embrace this subject and learn how to invest in the stock market myself. Thankfully, I was self-aware enough to know my limitations. I needed a financially intelligent approach to investing that offered low risk and fair returns that would allow me to sleep at night, knowing I wasn't being taken advantage of.

Large-Cap, Blue-Chip, Dividend-Paying Stocks

I DON'T have the attention span or expertise necessary to spend countless hours poring over the quarterly reports of publicly traded companies, attempting to divine their futures. Which is why my first serious foray into the stock market was mostly focused on large-cap, blue-chip, dividend-paying stocks that I trusted. For those not familiar with these terms:

- A *large-cap* company has a market capitalization of at least $10 billion. Market cap is calculated by multiplying the number of publicly traded shares in a company by the value of each of those shares. (If Company A issues one million shares and they trade for $1 each, then that company has a $1 million *market cap*.) At this writing, Apple is the largest company in the world by market cap at $1.52 trillion.

- *Blue chip* describes a large cap company with a long track record and an excellent reputation that *usually* also pays dividends. The size, strength, and dominance of these types of companies makes them highly liquid, which means you can buy or sell them easily. Also, because they are so large, and held by so many large funds and financial institutions, financial analysts watch them like a hawk. Every business decision they make, or major economic event, ends up being priced into the value of their shares.

- *Dividends* are a percentage of a company's profits distributed to shareholders, usually on a quarterly basis. The advantage of dividend-paying stocks is that you get "paid to wait." While your shares may go up and down in the short term, if they are chosen well, they should go up over the long term while you receive dividend income along the way.

My first major foray into the stock market began in the middle of the Great Recession from 2007 to 2009, which was triggered by a financial instrument, the mortgage-backed security or MBS, which most people knew nothing about at that time. Wall Street investment banks and aggressive mortgage companies had created an investment product made up of mortgages secured against single-family homes. Shares in those funds were sold to high net worth individuals, banks, and pension funds around the world on the strength of Wall Street's assurances that these mortgages were of the highest quality. Those promises were backed by the AAA rating that independent credit rating agencies had given them.

What the regulators and the rating agencies didn't know, until it was too late, was that the quality of the mortgages in these funds was not what they purported to be. Mortgage fraud on the grandest scale had occurred. Property appraisals had been fraudulently inflated. Borrowers' credit histories and employment income had been fabricated; minimum wage employees were found to have been buying $500,000 homes with no down payments. When people stopped making mortgage payments, the real estate bubble burst, triggering a global financial crisis on a scale never witnessed before.

When the smoke cleared, the financial carnage in the United States was devastating. Real estate values plummeted, erasing trillions of dollars in homeowner equity. Personal and corporate bankruptcies went through the roof. If there was an upside to the subprime crises, it was that the structural inefficiencies in the U.S. financial system that allowed this to happen in the first place were exposed in a way that made them impossible to ignore. The book *The Big Short* by Michael Lewis and the film of the same name starring Brad Pitt, Christian Bale, and Steve Carell do a brilliant and entertaining job of explaining how, why, and what triggered this financial debacle.[1]

In the midst of this financial crisis, when banks where failing, General Motors and Chrysler were both in bankruptcy, and the S&P 500 Index had fallen by 57%, I decided to focus more on the stock market. They say you should buy when others are selling and sell when others are buying. If that's true, my timing looked perfect.

Like all Canadians, I grew up banking at one of our country's six major financial institutions. Unlike the fragmented U.S. banking system, with its poorly regulated shadow-banking sector, Canada's system is highly concentrated, regulated, and watched by two ultra-conservative regulators, the Office of the Superintendent of Financial Institutions (OSFI) and the Financial Consumer Agency of Canada (FCAC). So, in the middle of the greatest financial crises of the twenty-first century, when banks around the world were failing or teetering on the brink of extinction,

Canada's banks proved to be the gold standard in governance and prudence.

Even though Canadian banks looked safe, in the middle of the crises, all shares in all banks were down. I didn't know much about the market at the time, or how to analyze a bank's financial statement, but as a Canadian I knew our system was an oligopoly—a monopoly shared by six banks. I also knew that monopolies are great things, if you own one. So, in March 2009, I bought shares in the Royal Bank of Canada for $32 each, 40% off their pre-crash high of $55. Dividends at that time were $2 per share annually, a 6.25% per annum yield.

Since then, the stock market has come roaring back to life. At the time of this writing, shares in the Royal Bank were trading at $108. Which is 340% more than I paid for them in 2009. In that same time, the dividends have increased from $2 to $4.20 per share. Which means I earn 13% per annum on my $32 shares in one of the most conservative banks in the world.

They say that when you invest in the stock market, it is a good idea to stick with companies that you know, understand, and believe in. So, when I bought my Royal Bank shares, I also invested in Canada's other five major banks—the Bank of Montreal, TD Canada Trust, Scotiabank, CIBC, and the National Bank of Canada. My reasoning was as simple as I am: in a small, wealthy, Western nation like Canada, the six institutions that share the country's banking monopoly have, through good times and bad, always done well. Buying shares in these banks was a proxy bet on the sovereign nation of Canada, which I know well and believe in.

Interestingly, one week before I made this investment, I was talked out of it by a shell-shocked money manager. At the height of the crisis, with the financial system in free fall, this man's day was spent watching the world fall apart on CNN and consoling clients. So, when I walked into his office wanting to buy bank stocks, he thought he was staring at a mad man.

Thankfully, I regained the courage of my convictions and bought my bank shares a week later.

A SIMPLE SUMMARY

- Make your own investment decisions.

- Large-cap, blue-chip, dividend-paying companies offer the safest *long-term* returns.

- Invest in companies you know, understand, and appreciate.

- Have the courage of your own convictions.

12

A Long-Term Strategy for the Know-Nothing Investor

I AM A BERKSHIRE HATHAWAY shareholder and have been for more than fifteen years. As a novice investor in the stock market, my decision to invest in Berkshire was simple. I concluded that if Warren Buffett was the greatest investor of all time, with a net worth of $71 billion, I should buy shares in his company. While most professional money managers would agree with my description of Buffett, they would be quick to point out that investing in one company at a time was stock picking, not a long-term strategy. And they would be right.

After investing in Canadian banks, Berkshire Hathaway, Apple, and a few other large, safe household names, I began running out of ideas. In fact, the more digging I did, the more confused I became. I soon realized how limited I was in my capacity. The financial world would always be too big, and the variables too great, for me to predict with any great degree of certainty what I should do next.

I needed a strategy, a financially intelligent approach to investing that would eliminate the risk of individual stocks, sectors, and manager selection. A way to make my money multiply, safely, over the long term and still sleep at night.

I tripped across the perfect strategy on page twenty of Berkshire Hathaway's 2013 annual report. In his letter to shareholders that year, Buffett argues that few investors and money managers have the skills necessary to predict a company's future earning power, that the goal of the know-nothing investor should not be to pick individual winners but to own a cross-section of the best American businesses, which are bound to do well in the long term. The best way to do that, he says, is to buy shares in something called an S&P 500 Index fund and hold on to them *forever*.[1]

When considering this type of investment, it is important to understand the difference between the S&P 500 Index and an *index fund*. The S&P 500 Index is a report card published by an independent reporting agency, S&P Dow Jones Indices. It tracks the performance of 500 of the strongest companies on the New York and NASDAQ stock exchanges. It is the standard that every money manager in the world is measured against. An index fund is different: it is a publicly traded mutual fund or ETF (exchange traded fund) constructed to mirror the S&P 500. The main advantage of this type of fund for the long-term, know-nothing investor is that it eliminates the risk of individual stocks, sectors, and manager selection. Instead of looking for a needle in a haystack, you are buying the haystack. Only overall market risk remains. The average annual growth rate of this index, since inception in 1926, has been 9.28%.

However, when investing, it is important to remember the *forever* part of Buffett's strategy. This is where the majority of investors go wrong. Dramatic, unpredictable economic events, "rogue waves," like the dot-com bubble of the 1990s or the subprime mortgage crises of 2008, will occur at unpredictable times. When this happens, you have to have the courage of your own convictions and not be distracted by the fear and greed that surrounds you. You never want to *have* to sell. So, if you are saving for a down payment on a home or income property, invest in guaranteed, interest-bearing government bonds or term deposits, instead of the stock market.

Buffett believes so strongly in investing in the S&P that he has directed his trustees to invest 90% of the money he leaves behind in S&P 500 Index funds and 10% in government bonds.[2] Since then, I have done the same.

Do Not Confuse Complex with Better

ANOTHER TYPE of investment that has become popular in recent years and that new investors should be wary of is a hedge fund. These investment vehicles were originally created for institutional investors and their high net worth clients. In recent years, the number of these types of funds has exploded and are marketed to retail investors.

Hedge funds have a very different strategy than index funds. They are the epitome of active trading. Their stated goal is to outperform the broader market (in other words, the S&P 500) by using various complex trading strategies that few people understand. They come in all sizes and shapes and can invest in almost anything, including real estate, stocks, commodities, options, derivatives, and debt. Bernard Madoff's Ponzi scheme, which I mentioned in chapter seven, posed as a legitimate hedge fund that employed a complex "split-strike conversion" strategy that no one understood to achieve returns that no one could replicate. Investors drawn into these funds often confuse complex with better, and the industry exploits this bias by charging higher fees for their wizardry. The standard is 2 and 20, meaning a 2% management fee, win or lose, every year, and a 20% performance fee (fund managers take 20% of all profits).

By contrast, the rules-based approach to portfolio construction of an S&P 500 Index *fund* that mirrors the S&P 500 *Index* eliminates discretion and the need to actively manage it. This dramatically reduces the fees and commissions paid to managers and financial institutions, boosting your returns. Vanguard, the fund Buffett recommends in his 2013 letter, has a management expense ratio of 0.03%.[3]

Buffett has spoken out against the exorbitant fees and practices of Wall Street often over the years, with little effect. By 2008, he had grown tired of not being heard and decided to draw attention to this issue by challenging the hedge fund industry with a $1 million bet. Surprisingly, the response to his challenge was initially muted. No one had the courage to take his bet. That was until Ted Seides of Protégé Partners LLC finally stepped forward, and the terms of the contest were agreed to: the growth of an S&P 500 Index fund versus a collection of five hedge funds from 2008 to 2018. Each of the five hedge funds were "funds of funds"; in other words, each fund collectively owned an interest in more than 200 of the best hedge funds on the market.

To make a long story short, Buffett won the bet, and the prize money was donated to a charity of his choosing— Girls Inc. of Omaha, Nebraska.

In those ten years, the S&P 500 had grown in value by 125.8%. The broad collection of well-selected hedge funds achieved only 36.3% in the same period. The bet also revealed three interesting facts:

- The S&P 500 generated returns 3.47 times higher than the top hedge funds.

- 60% of all gains achieved by the hedge funds were deducted for the fees.

- The hedge funds underperformed the S&P 500, *even on a gross level*—even if the fund managers had not charged their exorbitant 60% fees for their non-performance, the index fund was still a better investment.[4]

For most investors, the financial services industry is like a big casino where the house always wins. Investing in an S&P 500 Index fund through an online broker, like E*TRADE, Questrade, or TD Ameritrade, takes the house out of the picture and keeps their fees in your pocket— where they belong.

If an online account is not an attractive option for any reason, you can also open a *non-discretionary* account with any broker dealer. A non-discretionary account ensures *you* to make all decisions yourself.

How to Invest in S&P 500 Index Funds

S&P 500 Index funds are available around the world through major financial institutions and online brokers in a variety of major currencies. If you live outside of the United States, as I do, and want to invest in your home currency, many index funds employ hedging strategies at minimal additional cost. This eliminates the risk of your currency falling in value relative to the U.S. dollar.

Investing in a *hedged* S&P 500 fund as a non-U.S. resident *may* also be more tax efficient—eliminating U.S. withholding tax on the dividends you receive along the way.

There are several S&P 500 index funds to choose from today. The following three U.S.-dollar denominated funds have great track records worthy of consideration:

- Vanguard 500 Index (VFINX)
- SPDR S&P 500 (SPY)
- iShares Core S&P 500 (IVV)[5]

IF YOU are investing in Canada:

- Vanguard S&P 500 Index—CAD-hedged (VSP.TO)
- iShares Core S&P 500 Index—CAD-hedged (XSP.TO)

To learn more about S&P 500 Index funds, read *The Little Book of Common Sense Investing* by John C. Bogle, founder of the Vanguard Group of Investment Companies. Of Bogle, Buffett said, "If a statue is ever erected to honor the person who has done the most for American investors, the hands-down choice should be Jack Bogle."[6] High honor coming from the greatest investor in the world.

Investing Questions

BEFORE INVESTING, it is important to take some time to ask yourself some key questions:

- Should I invest in large-cap, dividend-paying, blue-chip stocks individually—or buy an S&P 500 Index fund?

- If I invest in individual stocks, which companies or sectors do I like and understand the most? Do I need to do more research—reading analyst and annual reports? Am I equipped and prepared to invest the time and energy necessary to monitor an individual company's performance and future prospects?

- If I invest in an S&P 500 Index fund, which one would be most cost efficient in terms of management fees? Do I know enough about the S&P 500, or should I study the subject more by reading *The Little Book of Common Sense Investing*?

A SIMPLE SUMMARY

- An S&P 500 Index fund eliminates the risk of individual stocks, sectors, and manager selection. Instead of looking for a needle in a haystack, you are buying the haystack.

- An S&P 500 Index fund will outperform most actively managed portfolios in the long run.

- It is important to never *have* to sell, especially if you're saving for a down payment on a home or income property.

- The financial services industry is like a big casino where the house always wins. An S&P 500 Index fund takes the house out of the picture and keeps the fees in your pocket—where they belong.

PART FOUR

The Financially Intelligent Entrepreneur

"In so many areas of life, you need to be a long-term optimist but a short-term realist."

CHESLEY B. SULLENBERGER, *HIGHEST DUTY*

13

Aviators and
Entrepreneurs

———

ON JANUARY 15, 2009, US Airways pilot Captain "Sully" Sullenberger's worst nightmare became a reality. Three minutes after takeoff from New York City's LaGuardia Airport, his Airbus A320 flew directly into a flock of Canadian geese and he lost thrust in both engines. Without power, he now had the unenviable task of landing a 500-ton glider on the Hudson River. The six o'clock news images of the huge aircraft floating, with wet and frightened passengers huddled on the wings, will be with me and millions of others forever.

I didn't know it at the time, but we were witnessing what would become known as "The Miracle on the Hudson"—the "miracle" moniker earned by the impossible odds of landing an Airbus A320 on a river in the most densely populated city in North America with no loss of life. What I found as remarkable as the happy ending enjoyed by the passengers that day were the close-up shots of Captain Sullenberger on dry land just after their rescue. Still in his pilot's uniform, white shirt and tie, he looked calm, cool, and collected. Just another day at the office for Sully.

In 2009, I didn't fully appreciate why Sullenberger could answer his call to duty so heroically that day. However, since then, I have watched Lise pursue her lifelong dream of becoming a single-engine pilot. In the process, I have come to realize that aviators and entrepreneurs have a lot more in common than I thought. They are both in the business of managing risk with a practiced calm.

Before she leaves for the airport, I watch Lise sit at our kitchen table and pore over charts and maps. Using ForeFlight software on her iPad, she plots a course over oceans and through mountain passes. She then calls FIC, the flight information center, and speaks to a meteorologist who gives her up-to-the-minute weather and air traffic reports. If the cloud cover, wind, or rain forecast are not optimal, she picks another route. Once she is confident that the data she has collected supports a safe flight, she drives to her flying club's hangar at the airport. There she pulls out a Cessna 180 and begins a preflight check of the aircraft. I have stood quietly, watching her go through the long list of visual, gas, and fluid-level checks before we sit in the aircraft. After starting the plane, she has another long list of gauges, incomprehensible to me, which she confirms are reading accurately. Once she is satisfied, then, and only then, do we taxi to the runway for takeoff.

When Lise is finally in the air, she knows there are risks, like bird strikes or mechanical failures, that she cannot eliminate. However, her training has prepared her for worst-case scenarios. She manages her altitude and flight path in a way that reduces those risks and allows her to land safely somewhere, no matter what happens.

Captain Sullenberger had forty-two years and 20,000 hours of experience, flying over one million passengers. He was a certified single-engine, multi-engine, and glider pilot instructor. When asked how he pulled off this nearly impossible feat, he said, "For forty-two years, I've been making small, regular deposits in this bank of experience, education, and training. And on January 15th, the balance was sufficient so I could make a very large withdrawal."[1]

STARTING, OWNING, and operating your own business is by far the single greatest wealth generator there is. The successful entrepreneur can parlay a small amount of capital, time, energy, and talent into a lifetime of income and large capital gains. Entrepreneurs also enjoy a creative freedom, independence, and sense of self-determination that they would not have working for someone else.

However, the entrepreneurial life, with its risks and responsibilities, is not for everyone. It can be all absorbing, and the mission-critical sense of urgency is hard to resist. Entrepreneurs often pour their hearts and souls into their businesses until they wake up one morning and realize that the ownership roles have been reversed.

Of course, going the extra mile is important. But it's not enough. The world is filled with hard-working, broke people. Successful entrepreneurs know they have to work *smart*, not just *hard*. They know that their growing business will always take more of them than they have to offer and that their family's emotional, physical, and spiritual health needs to be a priority. Divorce is the single greatest destroyer of personal wealth there is. If your marriage suffers, your family and your business will suffer with it.

The financially intelligent entrepreneur understands this and learns how to manage risk, create boundaries, and live within the tension of competing demands. They are single-minded and passionate about their businesses, but their identities and *personal* financial lives do not get lost in the process. They understand that a business is a separate legal personality, an entity with a life of its own, and that the same financially intelligent principles apply to a business that apply to their personal lives. A business must save, control, multiply, and protect its assets. It should also own its own real estate, if the business model supports it. Entrepreneurs must also be persistent, determined, and self-aware—able to embrace short-term sacrifice for long-term gain.

A SIMPLE SUMMARY

- Owning your own business can be one of the greatest wealth generators there is.

- Success as an entrepreneur is about managing risk with a practiced calm.

- A business is a separate legal personality. Don't confuse its life with your own.

- You have to work hard and smart, and remember that your physical, emotional, and spiritual health need to be a priority.

14

You Don't Know
What You Don't Know

FRED IS A close friend who came to me a few years ago for some business advice. He had been working in the corporate headquarters of a major travel agency franchisor with hundreds of locations across North America for ten years. His senior-level management position paid a generous six-figure salary with bonuses and benefits. There had been a recent merger with a large publicly traded company and the corporate culture was changing. Opportunities for advancement were not as promising as they had been in the past.

Before joining the company, Fred had been a partner in a small but successful family business and was considering taking the entrepreneurial leap again, but he wasn't sure. He was looking for a friend's objective feedback. When I asked what type of business he was thinking of getting into, he talked about buying a franchise in the company he worked for. He was considering one of the most profitable, well-run locations in the network. He knew the owner well and had already had soft discussions about a sale in the $575,000 price range. The fact that it was a profitable, well-run franchise was a plus and a minus.

The pluses were a solid recurring revenue of $5.8 million, a $200,000-a-year bottom line, a strong customer base, and a dedicated staff. The minuses were the high cost, uncertain upside potential, and down payment. A top-producing franchise demands a higher price, and it was doing so well already that Fred wasn't sure he could grow the bottom line and increase the business's value. Also, while the owner was prepared to carry $375,000 in financing, Fred would still have to come up with $200,000 from his retirement savings account. Was it worth the risk?

Risk is an entrepreneur's best friend. Knowledge and expertise can reduce your downside and supercharge your returns, and in this case, Fred had both. It was his job at corporate headquarters to train and motivate franchisees. He spoke at conferences all over the world and had worked with the most successful operators. He knew what worked and what didn't. No one was better trained or equipped to buy a franchise in this travel agency network than Fred. I believed this, and I told him so.

Three years ago, Fred resigned from his job at corporate headquarters and took the leap. Since then, he has increased sales 100%, from $5.8 million to $11.9 million, and the bottom line from $200,000 to $400,000 a year. The business he bought for $575,000 is now worth $1.2 million and he has paid off the $375,000 in seller-financing.

Fred had the training and experience necessary to run a franchise. But he also had the self-awareness and humility to know that "sometimes you don't know what you don't know," until it's too late. We all have blind spots. Which is why it is important to do your due diligence and seek objective feedback from people whose opinions you respect, people who care enough to tell you what they really think, not what you want to hear.

Always Have an Open Mind

I RECEIVED another request for my feedback about a business opportunity from a friend of a friend a few years ago. This gentleman and his business partner planned on buying a number of physiotherapy clinics from retiring therapists. However, neither he nor his partner were physiotherapists themselves, nor had they ever worked in the industry. Only one of the partners lived in the region they were targeting, and he was fully employed already. This new scheme would be in addition to his already demanding, full-time day job. The icing on the cake was that they had *no money of their own*. They were looking for investors. That was the real reason for his email.

After reading the proposal, I gave him some feedback, which was polite and honest but not supportive. What I received in response was an angry defense of his idea. He wasn't looking for my opinion. He was looking for people to agree with his. I heard later that the scheme ultimately failed, taking a lot of people's savings with it. I knew this gentleman's email had been a roundabout way of asking me to invest. But I answered his question honestly because I wanted to protect him and his investors, if I could.

Surrounding yourself with agreeable people condemns you to a prison of your own ideas. Great people won't share great thinking if they are not heard. Honor and embrace disagreement. The final decision is yours. But at least it's made with your eyes wide open.

Pride Comes before the Fall

ANOTHER FRIEND of mine, Allan, is a retired math teacher, baseball coach, and Boy Scout leader. He is also one of the nicest men you will ever meet. So, when he called and asked for some advice, I quickly agreed. The man who showed up at Starbucks that afternoon wasn't the Allan I had always known and loved. His ready smile and positive energy were gone. He looked like he hadn't slept in days. As his story unfolded, I understood why.

It turns out that, not long after retiring, Allan and his brother-in-law, Armando, had bought an auto glass franchise together. Because of a previous business failure, Armando had no cash or credit. But he assured Allan he knew how to run a glass shop; he had grown up in his family's business in Brazil. Based on these assurances, Allan agreed that Armando could earn his interest in the business by running the day-to-day operations. Armando had no other income, so it was also agreed that he would take a small salary to cover his living expenses, until they were profitable. Allan invested the start-up capital and signed personal guarantees.

At the time, it sounded like a great deal. Allan had $300,000 in retirement savings and an excellent credit rating. He could handle the $100,000 franchise fee and the $50,000 start-up capital with room to breathe. The franchisor could not guarantee earnings, but they projected $200,000 a year for a well-run franchise.

Unfortunately, things did not go as planned. Two weeks into the partnership, Allan popped in unannounced at 11 a.m. The lights were out, and the doors were locked. The posted opening hour was 8 a.m. Allan was concerned so he called Armando, who answered on the fifth ring with a groggy "Hello." He had slept in. To add to his disappointment, Allan also learned over the phone that morning that the $50,000 in start-up costs that they had budgeted for had ballooned to $150,000. Armando blamed the landlord. However, it was later revealed that Armando's budgeting errors for leasehold improvements were the cause of the shortfall.

Allan does not handle conflict well. So instead of confronting these issues head-on, he kept his feelings to himself, put on a happy face, and pressed on. Things went from bad to worse. Armando wasn't only incompetent and lazy; he was dishonest. In addition to the small salary he was pulling from the unprofitable business, he was stealing cash out of the till. When confronted, he insisted he was not stealing. As a partner, he was *borrowing* money for a family emergency.

Inconsistencies, inefficiencies, and excuses followed Armando everywhere he went. The business was losing money. Allan invested his life savings until they were gone. Rent and a long list of bills were overdue. In a last-ditch attempt to save the business, they refinanced some equipment and borrowed $50,000 at rate of 15% per year.

A loan that Allan personally guaranteed, because of course Armando had no credit.

Allan had no experience running a business of his own and thought he was solving this problem by taking in a partner. When the business failed, their relationship failed with it. Thanksgiving dinners with his in-laws became tense. Allan's wife did not know how much they had lost, and he didn't know how to tell her.

My friend shared all of this with tears in his eyes. I had tears in mine. He was looking to me for answers, and I had none. I was flabbergasted by his lack of common sense. If he had called me for an opinion before he decided to invest, I would have advised him to run for the hills.

NOTE THE differences between Fred's and Allan's approaches to their decision-making. Fred, an experienced entrepreneur and expert in the travel agency franchise business, came to me and another entrepreneur and trusted friend before committing financially. He transparently shared his thinking, his financial position, his goals, and his dreams, and he asked for objective feedback. Fred is self-aware and humble enough to know that he may have been missing something. He received the confirmation he needed from people he trusted and respected, and he hit a home run.

Allan, who had no experience in business, didn't reach out to me or anyone else before he took the leap and gambled away his retirement fund. I would have learned enough in a three-minute telephone call to advise him against this scheme. So, what happened? Why didn't Allan reach out for help?

I am not a psychologist or a mind reader, so I cannot say for sure. But if I had to guess I would say it was likely pride. As I have said before, Allan is one of the nicest men you will ever meet. But as a respected leader in the community, he may have felt uncomfortable coming to me and opening up about his financial life. So now, in his retirement, when he should be enjoying the fruits of a life well lived, he is dealing with bankruptcy and major marital issues.

THE SUCCESSFUL entrepreneur and aviator both know that no matter how much talent, skill, and discipline they have, variables like a bird strike, an engine failure, the economy, or competition are totally out of their control. They know that their jobs are to reduce, confine, and eliminate as much risk from their adventure as possible. My friend Fred succeeded in the travel business because he knew how important his preflight checks were. My friend Allan crashed and burned because he climbed into a plane blindfolded, with his incompetent brother-in-law at the controls.

A SIMPLE SUMMARY

- Everyone has blind spots. Be humble and seek counsel from people you trust—before investing in a business.

- Encourage people to challenge your opinions.

- Decide how much you are prepared to invest and stick to your guns. Your business will always want more than you have, or want, to give it.

15

When You Mix Business with Pleasure, Business Always Wins

―――――

MANY NEW BUSINESS OWNERS are drawn to the idea of having a partner to share their work, risk, and investment with. There is an exciting esprit de corps that comes with every new venture and it is nice to share that with someone you know and trust.

The Entrepreneurs' Organization (EO) is an international network of entrepreneurs that I belonged to for years. When thinking about the pluses and minuses of partnerships, I reflect on an exchange I witnessed at one of our learning events that has always stuck with me. A visiting mentor/entrepreneur was sharing his personal "lessons from the edge" with our group one evening. When he was asked his view on partnerships, he made his position clear: "I don't believe in partnerships. They never work. They are not worth the risk."

I will never forget the incredulous look on the face of an EO member sitting next to me when he heard this. Visibly taken aback by the boldness of the speaker's remarks, he shot his hand up into the air immediately. When finally called upon, my neighbor, Bill, launched into his defense. Sounding angry and hurt, he said, "I totally disagree with what you have just said. I have a great partner. We are best friends, and our strengths complement each other."

Our speaker listened patiently as Bill continued on about his partnership made in heaven. When he finally ran out of steam, our speaker politely acknowledged Bill's right to his opinion and then said that he stood by his remarks. As I watched this exchange unfold, I politely said nothing, but I agreed with our speaker that evening and I still do. Of course, there are exceptions to every rule, but in my experience most business partnerships ultimately fail in one way or another.

In an interesting twist of fate, a few years after that EO event, my partner-loving friend Bill called me with a business proposal. When we eventually sat down to get caught up, he launched into an angry tirade about the partner that he had so passionately defended a few years earlier. Bill was raising money to buy him out.

The idea of partnership is appealing to the new entrepreneur; the reality is almost always different. Inequities—perceived or real—foster resentment. Some partners get along well themselves but go home to critical spouses who sow seeds of division that eventually take root. Partnerships made in heaven often end in finger-pointing, acrimony, lawsuits, and divorce. Lifelong friends and families are torn apart. When you mix business with pleasure, business *always* wins.

Whenever possible, employ people to backfill your weaknesses, instead of tying yourself to an uncertain future with a partner. Partnership is a risk you can eliminate easily by not having one.

Partnership Agreements

THERE ARE certain types of professional practices, like law and accounting, that are built on partnership structures. If you are in one of these professions, or in another industry and have decided to take on partnership risk, make sure to engage a lawyer who specializes in this area and have a partnership agreement in place. Like a prenuptial agreement, it anticipates your eventual separation and defines the terms of that separation in advance. Of course, discussing this during the honeymoon phase of a partnership is not fun, which is why many people avoid the subject altogether and end up paying for it later. Having an agreement in place can make a stressful situation bearable and protects the underlying value of your business.

A SIMPLE SUMMARY

- Having a partner sounds great, but the reality is often different.

- If you value a relationship with someone, don't go into business with them.

- Partnership issues can destroy a perfectly good business. Not having a partner is the simplest way to avoid that risk.

- If you have to have a partner, invest in a quality partnership agreement.

16

Risk Management

———————

A VACANCY CAUSED BY a tenant going out of business is one example of a risk that all landlords take that cannot be fully controlled. We had a big-box-retailer tenant that sold camping, hunting, and fishing gear. The retail chain was owned by a multi-billion-dollar investment fund with a one-hundred-year history, so we were confident in their ability to live up to the terms of their lease. Then one day, a major U.S. competitor moved into the market. A year later, the lights were out, and our tenant was gone.

When a tenant stops paying rent, the first thing you do as a landlord is reacquaint yourself with the guarantee clause in your lease. In this case, the multi-billion-dollar parent company that owned the store had given a guarantee for the first two years. After that, the retailer was responsible for its own financial obligations. We had no legal right to pursue the wealthy parent company that owned them, but they would have to prove that in court.

To avoid this expense, the company chose to negotiate partial payouts with their landlords. They were pleasant and professional to deal with.

While I was disappointed by the vacancy, I didn't feel bad or taken advantage of. Those are the rules of the game when you deal with a *limited liability company*. We knew the terms of the lease when we bought the property, and we were happy to play by them.

The Limited Liability Company

IF YOU are one of those people lucky enough to be born in a Western nation, regardless of how rich or poor you are today, you are a winner in the lottery of life. Being born in the West means you live in a nation with an evolved rule of law that governs the ownership of real estate, intellectual property, and the legal concept of the limited liability company. Taken for granted by most of us, these invisible legal mechanisms, and their enforcement, are all that separate us from the poverty and corruption that people in less developed countries are forced to endure.

The origin of the limited liability company goes back to seventeenth-century England, when Queen Elizabeth I granted a royal charter to the East India Company. This allowed the company to sell shares in trading expeditions to wealthy aristocrats, without the owners risking personal liability if a ship were lost at sea. The limited liability company is a separate legal personality, distinct from its owner. When you see the words *Limited*, *Incorporated*, or

Corporation (or the corresponding abbreviations *Ltd.*, *Inc.*, and *Corp.*) after a company's name, it is a public declaration that the financial responsibilities of that business are limited to the assets of the company.

If you own an interest in a limited liability company, all the assets you personally hold, apart from your business, are out of reach of your company's creditors. This freedom to invest, without the fear of personal liability, fuels our stock markets and encourages business and private investment at all levels. By contrast, sole proprietors have unlimited liability for the debts of the business they own. So, when I started out again after my bankruptcy, I followed in the wise footsteps of those seventeenth-century aristocrats and the East India Company and compartmentalized my risk, and family's assets, by incorporating every business I started.

I always worked hard and believed in what I was doing, but I took a less emotional, more calculated approach to my endeavors. If, for reasons out of my control, an idea didn't deliver the profits or potential I needed to justify my investment, I let it go and moved on to my next great adventure.

Incorporating your business is the least expensive risk-mitigating insurance policy you can buy. If you own multiple businesses, incorporating each of them separately creates a firewall between you and your business affairs. It allows you to contain and quantify the risk you take in each new venture.

Contingent Liabilities

ANY GOOD lawyer will tell you that the money you invest in the company is not the only risk you take when you operate a business. If you are a director of a corporation and your company is sued for any one of a number of reasons, sometimes completely out of your control, you can be held personally responsible. If an employee is negligent, breaks the law, or runs afoul of industry regulations, directors can be sued. These are referred to as *contingent liabilities*. Insurance companies sell insurance to help reduce this exposure, but they cannot cover all risks.

If you are married, one popular way of reducing this risk is to maintain the savings and assets you want to protect in your spouse's name. If they are not a director of the company, they can't be held responsible for its legal issues. Lise always held title to our homes, rental properties, and the savings we were not prepared to risk.

Count the Cost

WHEN RUNNING a cash-hungry business, the temptation to fund its growth is great.

Imagine this scenario: you have worked long and hard to make your dream a reality. Business is booming. You need a new piece of equipment, a larger space, and more staff to service the customers beating down your door.

As a financially intelligent entrepreneur, you have committed as much of your personal savings to the venture as you are prepared to at this time. You have agreed with yourself that the money in your 10% savings account is off-limits. So instead, you walk into your local banker's office and ask for a business loan. You quickly discover that your business doesn't have a long-enough track record of earnings or assets for the bank to lend it money. However, the banker smiles and says you have equity in your home and a great credit rating, and they would be happy to give you a line of credit or a second mortgage on your home. Since you have agreed not to borrow against your home, which you consider a part of your 10% account, that is not an option, but the line of credit sounds good. Before you decide to take that line of credit, it is important to understand that your personal guarantee on that line of credit, or on any equipment you might lease for your business, is *personal*. If things do not go as planned and your business cannot pay it off, you—not your business—will be responsible for 100% of those payments.

Many borrowers also misunderstand the obligations of cosigning a loan. Cosigning does not reduce your exposure. The lender can hold individual co-guarantors responsible for the entire amount of the loan, regardless of how many borrowers have guaranteed it.

There Is No Life Like It

AS AN ambitious young man, I believed that my reasons for wanting to be an entrepreneur were purely financial. However, over the years, I have taken various predictive tests—the DISC assessment, StrengthsFinder, and Kolbe to name a few. Every test I have taken shows a classic entrepreneur personality profile. I now realize that, rich or poor, win or lose, I would have always chosen this life. It is how I am wired.

Starting in my early twenties, I jumped from one "great" business idea to the next in search of my million-dollar opportunity. Most were direct-sales related. After going through personal bankruptcy in 1989, I continued pursuing my dreams, but I was far more risk averse. If the long-term prospects of an idea didn't look good, I would change directions quickly. I looked at the businesses I started the same way employees look at their jobs. I always saved at least 10% of the salary I paid myself and invested in real estate. Our new financially intelligent way of life and 10% account were our plan A. I saw my businesses as a form of employment. If I hit my home run, great; if not, no problem. We would save and invest in real estate and be fine in the long run either way.

In 1994, I started a small loan company with one employee. I grew that business into one of the largest online payday loan companies in the United States, employing 500 people and issuing millions of dollars in $300 loans every month. Ten years later, in 2004, I finally hit my home run when I sold that business to my management team. Using the proceeds from that sale, I became a full-time investor in commercial income-producing real estate and large-cap publicly traded equities, which I buy and hold *forever*. The only operating business we own today is the Sportsplex arena in our community. I delegate the day-to-day operations of the facility to a management team. This leaves us free to travel and get involved in the great causes we care most about. It also gives me the time I need to explore new sides of myself, like writing this book.

The entrepreneurial life has been good to me. There is really no life like it.

A SIMPLE SUMMARY

- Incorporating creates a firewall between your personal finances and your business. It is the lowest-cost insurance policy a business owner has.

- Reduce risk by keeping assets in your spouse's name.

- Living a financially intelligent life by saving and investing for your family's future should always be your plan A. If your business does well, great. If it doesn't, you will be fine in the long run.

Conclusion:
A Force for Good

———

THE LOUD BUZZER gave me access to the shelter through a heavy metal door. As I stepped inside, the antiseptic odors stung my nostrils. Lonely, empty faces stared up as I passed. I took a deep breath. *I can do this.*

Triage is the name of an emergency shelter in Vancouver's Downtown Eastside. This area is widely known as Canada's poorest postal code, and it is infamous for its open-air drug market. The neighborhood explodes into what locals call "Mardi Gras" on welfare days. For many people, it is the last stop on the way out of mainstream society, and most never return.

The saddest players in this tragic comedy are the mentally ill. They end up at the shelter as a result of an indifferent government's failed attempts to support them in the community, instead of in institutions. Alone on the streets, these most vulnerable citizens are easy prey for hustlers, pimps, and drug dealers.

As a recent donor, I had been invited by Triage for a tour of the facility. Leslie, the shelter manager, was a passionate lady in her mid-thirties who knew these streets from the other side of the counter.

As we walked, she told me about Triage's transitional housing strategy and how the shelter was the starting point, a short-stay facility designed to stabilize the tenants and prepare them for independent living elsewhere. Half listening, I nodded, feeling oddly voyeuristic as I peered into the empty cinderblock rooms. The walls were painted drab yellow. Metal bedframes were bolted to the concrete walls and covered with thin, plastic-coated mattresses. I couldn't help but think of how many places like this my mother had called home.

My mother had fought a lifelong battle with mental illness. My father's sudden death from complications due to diabetes in 1983, when I was twenty-three, had left her alone. With the only sane anchor in her life gone, she went downhill quickly. Every attempt by my brothers and me to help her over the years had failed. She became highly transient, moving from city to city without any rhyme or reason. Her homes were rooming houses, emergency shelters, psychiatric wards, and sometimes jail. She finally died alone in a rooming house in Halifax, Nova Scotia, in 1999 and was buried in a pauper's grave before we knew.

When my tour of the shelter was over, we adjourned to Leslie's office for a cup of coffee. We relaxed as I told her my mother's story. She listened with an empathy that only someone who trades in these stories can have.

My visit to the shelter that day began as an attempt to reconcile my past with my new financial reality. My whole adult life had been focused on survival and success. In the past, I had been generous with family and friends but spent little time thinking of anyone else. I was discovering that money used correctly is a powerful change agent. And that money for the sake of money was a hollow pursuit. That day was a turning point in my spiritual journey and the start of a new, more generous way of living. Today, much of our time, energy, and financial resources are focused on giving back. My only regret is that I did not discover this more meaningful, generous way of life earlier.

People often say they want to "do something." If you are feeling that tug in your heart but don't know where to start, my advice is to lean into causes that mean the most to you. Start small, and don't give up. I am sure you will find giving back as meaningful and addictive as Lise and I have.

If you are starting out and not in a position to give a lot financially, give of yourself. Your time, energy, and talents are valuable and rewarding to give. Giving back will give you a *why* for the discipline of your new financially intelligent way of life.

AS I mentioned in the introduction, I wrote this book for my children and my children's children. When I am gone and they wonder, "What would Dad do?" they will know. I also wrote this book for anyone feeling as lost and trapped as I was as a young man. I know how fearful and desperate you are feeling. But remember no matter who you are or where you are from, success is not a function of your IQ, academic achievement, or family background. It is a combination of age-old financial wisdom and knowledge, guided by emotional intelligence—persistence, determination, motivation, self-awareness, and the ability to embrace short-term sacrifice for long-term gain. If you have failed miserably in these areas of your life in the past, do not be discouraged. Your level of emotional and financial intelligence, or FQ, can be developed over time. You can live a life filled with options and opportunities, instead of regrets and debts.

Do not be fooled by the simplicity of these timeless truths. Truth is always simple. If you can read these words, you can apply them.

Embrace these ideas. Make them your own. They changed our lives, and they will change your life forever.

Acknowledgments

_____

WANT TO THANK Lise, my beautiful wife of thirty years. *Simple Wealth* is *our* story.

Many thanks to Franco Papalia, who shared his family's heartwarming journey of struggle and success, and my good friend Lance Bracken—your story of life in the hills is humbling and awe-inspiring.

I would also like to thank my two close friends and fellow entrepreneurs Craig Faulkner and Fred Mercer. Together we are popularly known as the Three Amigos. I couldn't imagine doing life without you guys.

Finally, no acknowledgment would be complete without me thanking the richest friend I have. He owns all the cattle on all the hills and is the author of all that is good and right in me.

Thank you, God, you are the Lord of my life.

Notes

Introduction

1. George S. Clason, *The Richest Man in Babylon* (New York: Penguin Random House, [1926] 2019), 27.

Part One epigraph

Daniel Goleman, *Emotional Intelligence: Why It Can Matter More Than IQ*, 10th anniversary ed. (New York: Bantam Dell, 2005), 34.

1. Academic Achievement Is Being Oversold

1. Daniel Goleman, *Emotional Intelligence: Why It Can Matter More Than IQ*, 10th anniversary ed. (New York: Bantam Dell, 2005), 34.
2. Ibid., 34.

3. A Partial Truth Is No Truth at All

1. Your Mental Wealth, "Money Scripts," yourmentalwealthadvisors .com/money-scripts.
2. 1 Tim. 6:10 (New International Version).
3. Randy Alcorn, *Money, Possessions, and Eternity* (Carol Stream, IL: Tyndale House, 2003).

Part Two epigraph

George S. Clason, *The Richest Man in Babylon* (New York: Penguin Random House, [1926] 2019), 3.

5. Proven Principle #2: Control

1. Travis Bradberry and Jean Greaves, *Emotional Intelligence 2.0* (San Diego, CA: TalentSmart, 2009).

7. Proven Principle #4: Protect

1. Charles Sizemore, "Want to Avoid a Portfolio Blow Up? Don't Forget Warren Buffett's Two Rules," *Forbes*, November 3, 2011, forbes.com/sites/moneybuilder/2011/11/03/want-to-avoid-a-portfolio-blow-up-dont-forget-warren-buffetts-two-rules/#7e 4244d063ad.
2. Barnini Chakraborty, "Bernie Madoff Billionaire Ponzi Scheme and What He Wants Now: Everything You Should Know," FoxNews.com, March 9, 2020, foxnews.com/us/bernie-madoff-ponzi-scheme-everything-you-should-know.

8. Proven Principle #5: Own

1. Donald R. Haurin, Toby L. Parcel, and R. Jean Haurin, "Does Home Ownership Affect Child Outcomes?" *Real Estate Economics* 30, no. 4 (February 2002): 635–66, doi.org/10.1111/1540-6229 .t01-2-00053.

Part Three epigraph

Mark Twain, *Following the Equator: A Journey around the World* (New York: Doubleday & McClure Co., 1897), 535.

11. Make the Market Your Friend

1. Michael Lewis, *The Big Short: Inside the Doomsday Machine* (New York: W.W. Norton & Company, 2010); Adam McKay (dir.), *The Big Short* (Hollywood, CA: Paramount Pictures, 2015).

12. A Long-Term Strategy
for the Know-Nothing Investor

1. Warren Buffet, "Chairman's Letter," *Berkshire Hathaway Inc. 2013 Annual Report*, 2014, berkshirehathaway.com/2013ar/2013 ar.pdf.

2. Ibid.

3. For a list of all 500 companies currently held, see "Vanguard 500 Index Fund Investor Shares," Vanguard, investor.vanguard .com/mutual-funds/profile/VFINX.

4. Gregor Zupanac, "Three Very Important Lessons to Learn from Warren Buffett's $1 Million Bet," Solidum Capital, October 10, 2018, blog.solidum.capital/three-very-important-lessons-to-learn-from-warren-buffetts-1-million-bet-7111b3368f11.

5. Kent Thune, "The Best S&P 500 Index Funds," *The Balance*, December 10, 2019, thebalance.com/best-sandp-500-index-funds-2466399.

6. John C. Bogle, *The Little Book of Common Sense Investing: The Only Way to Guarantee Your Fair Share of Stock Market Returns*, 10th anniversary ed. (Hoboken, NJ: Wiley, 2017); John Melloy, "Warren Buffett Says Jack Bogle Did More for the Individual Investor Than Anyone He's Ever Known," CNBC.com, January 16, 2019, cnbc.com/2019/01/16/warren-buffett-says-jack-bogle-did-more-for-the-individual-investor-than-anyone-hes-ever-known.html.

Part Four epigraph

Chesley B. Sullenberger with Jeffrey Zaslow, *Highest Duty: My Search for What Really Matters* (New York: HarperCollins, 2009), 119.

13. Aviators and Entrepreneurs

1. David F. Osborne, *Five Minutes to Impact: The Final Flight of the Comanche* (Greenville, SC: Ambassador International, 2017), 2.

AUTHOR PHOTO: MARTIN DEE

About the Author

———

DAVID ASH IS a career entrepreneur and full-time investor. He is a founding member of TIGER 21's Vancouver, BC, chapter, a global, peer-to-peer learning network of high net worth individuals, managing $75 billion in personal assets. He is a past recipient of the Kaufmann Foundation's Community Service Award for his work at the Vivian, a transitional housing program for Vancouver's hardest of hard to house women, named after his mother. David is also the author of *Goodness Is Contagious: From Profit to Purpose*, his life story.